ISBN: 978-1-57972-990-5
Printed in the United States of America

TABLE OF CONTENTS

APPENDIX

A NOTE FROM CHUCK SWINDOLL

Let's be honest.

For most of us, certain parts of the Bible—especially in the Old Testament—can be hard to understand. The emphasis given to slaughtering animals, building altars, and personal cleanliness can be downright confusing. And then there are all the violent conflicts, commands to destroy entire cities, and chapters of mind-numbing (dare I say, *boring*?) genealogies. All these can leave us in a stupor!

As we read the ancient Book, we encounter stories, names, and traditions that were commonplace to folks back then . . . but they sound peculiar to our modern-day ears. Questions quickly come to mind.

What's the role of a Levite?

Why does the Old Testament talk so much about sacrifices?

Why did the Israelites celebrate feasts?

The answers to these questions—and so many more—are important. If we miss the Old Testament's cultural context, we may overlook vital lessons about God's character. What's more, we will fail to understand truth that can change our lives.

The book you hold in your hand, *Insight's Handbook of Old Testament Backgrounds: Key Customs from Each Book, Genesis–Esther*, is a great place to start. With answers to common questions about biblical culture and short articles on interesting topics, this handbook will help you understand the cultural context of the first seventeen books of the Bible.

My hope is that this practical resource will guide you to a greater understanding of the Old Testament . . . and ultimately, to a deeper relationship with our God who inspired it.

May God teach and encourage you as you study His Word.

Charles R. Swindoll

HOW TO USE THIS BOOK

Plan to use this volume alongside your copy of Scripture. We have organized the topics by the verse and Bible book in which they appear. Many Bible books cover the same topics, so in an effort to avoid repetition, we've included both a **Scripture index** and a **subject index**. So when some detail from, say, Genesis, strikes you, search our indexes in the back of the book to see where we've dealt with the topic. We hope you'll find this a helpful way to explore the wide array of interesting Bible backgrounds and cultural insights presented in this book.

INSIGHT'S *Handbook*
OF OLD TESTAMENT
BACKGROUNDS

GENESIS–ESTHER

GENESIS

—❦—

2:19–20   Hello, My Name Is . . .

It's a practice that occurs millions of times a day . . . every day. The practice is so ingrained in humanity, we've been doing it since the days of Adam. We name things. We name places, and we name people.

In the Old Testament, a name was more than a mere tag of identification—it served to communicate something about the nature of the person. To blot out someone's name "from under heaven" was to remove all remembrance of that individual's existence—to lose him or her in the forgotten corners of history (Deuteronomy 7:24; 9:14).

Ancient parents chose names for their children based not on popularity or personal preference but on a desire to memorialize important events or to reveal perceived or prescribed character. A name, therefore, established one's reputation. This was certainly the case for Isaac (Genesis 21:3, 6), Jacob and Esau (25:25–26; 27:36), and Joseph (30:23–24). Equally significant and common, renaming represented a change in an individual's character and a new beginning, as it did for Joseph when he became prime minister of Egypt (41:45).

In the Old Testament, naming was sometimes a way of declaring ownership or authority over someone, some place, or something. This was certainly true when the one naming gave his or her personal name to a location, as David did in 2 Samuel 12:28 or as the Lord did in Jeremiah 7:10–12. However, this was not the case with Adam and the animals. God had already given Adam and Eve dominion over His creation (Genesis 1:26), so Adam's naming the animals was an exercise of recognizing the character of each creature and establishing the kind of relationship that would exist between humans and beasts.

Related passages: Genesis 17:3–5, 15; 32:27–28; Daniel 1:7; Matthew 16:17–18; Acts 13:9

11:4–5 Making a Name for Ourselves

Stubborn pride marks human nature. So do curiosity and a desire to create. These human characteristics mixed together in one of the most enigmatic stories in the Bible—the building of the Tower of Babel.

Towers in the ancient world were common structures. Built into the walls of cities or placed in vineyards, watchtowers served as lookouts. But there was a special class of towers built for the purpose of worship— ziggurats. Ancient ziggurats were rectangular structures, built in stages

with sun-dried (sometimes glazed), mud bricks in a stair-stepped pattern. Ziggurats usually included an inclining ramp or staircase along each side, and because they were used for religious ceremonies, they were often topped with a temple that housed sacred objects or images.

An ancient ziggurat

Ziggurats didn't have to be extraordinarily tall to attract attention, especially on the flat, open plain of the Euphrates Valley (ancient Shinar; Genesis 11:2)—the most likely location of the Tower of Babel. No precise measurements of the Tower of Babel exist, though some scholars estimate the tower's height might have exceeded 295 feet. Regardless of how tall it actually was, the intention of the builders was to construct a tower "whose top [would] reach into heaven" (11:4). In other words, they wanted to build the tower large enough and tall enough to be seen for miles and thereby establish their reputation as a great people.

In one sense, the people who built the Tower of Babel got their wish—their reputation was established. However, it was a reputation as a proud and rebellious people, not a great people. Further, the city and tower they built on the plain of Shinar was meant to prevent the world's population from dispersing, in direct defiance of God's command (Genesis 9:1). And for that they were judged.

Related passages: Judges 9:51–52; Psalm 61:3; Proverbs 18:10; Luke 14:28

17:9–14 A Delicate Procedure

It might come as a surprise to many, but circumcision, the cutting off of the foreskin of the penis, wasn't practiced exclusively by the Hebrews. Many people practiced circumcision in the ancient world—Moabites, Ammonites, Edomites, and Egyptians. The uncircumcised included Canaanites, Philistines, and the people of Mesopotamia—Assyrians, Babylonians, and Persians.

Why the Moabites, Ammonites, and Edomites practiced circumcision is unknown. But the Egyptians practiced it as a rite of passage, either from boyhood to manhood or from being single to being married. Generally, all Egyptian priests were circumcised.

Circumcision for Hebrew males was more significant than a rite of passage or a tribal mark. It was a sign of faith in God and an agreement to uphold the covenant relationship with Him. God commanded that every male child from Abraham's progeny be circumcised on the eighth day after birth. Adult males who refused circumcision or refused to have their sons circumcised were cut off from the community of faith and cast outside the covenant.

Hebrews practiced circumcision from the time of Abraham through the years of their bondage in Egypt. The practice appears to have been interrupted during the wilderness wandering (Joshua 5:2–9), but from the time of Joshua to the present day, Jewish males have been and continue to be circumcised as a sign of their covenant with God.

Related passages: Genesis 17:23–27; 34:15–25; Romans 4:11

18:1–10   Strike the Tent

From the earliest times, the Bible records men and women living in houses in and around cities. The people of the Shinar plain used sun-dried, mud bricks to build a city and a great tower, Abraham came from the city of Ur, and Lot and his family moved into the immoral city of Sodom. But the most common form of dwelling, and the one Abraham and his descendants lived in until their conquest of the Promised Land under Joshua, was a tent—the perfect dwelling for nomads.

Ancient tents, not unlike tents used today by the Bedouin in the Middle East, were woven together from goat's hair and stretched over supporting poles, with the tent's edges tied to wooden pegs driven into the ground. Tent sizes varied according to the number of occupants. As a family grew, new sections were added and divided into private quarters by means of curtains. For wealthy and polygamous shepherds, such as Jacob, each wife might have had her own tent.

In the Old Testament, women were responsible for the weaving, repairing, and pitching of tents. However, in the New Testament, the apostle Paul's profession was that of a tent-maker (Acts 18:1–3).

Tents also appear symbolically in Scripture. Tents are likened to the shortness of life (Isaiah 38:12), to the description of the heavens (Psalm 104:2), and to the place of safety and righteousness (Job 5:24; 11:14; 22:23).

Related passages: Genesis 4:20; 31:33; Judges 4:21; Isaiah 54:2; 2 Corinthians 5:1, 4

Tent dwelling

24:2–9; 47:29   I Promise

Remember when one person could trust another based only on a promise? "He's as good as his word," people used to say. Only a promise and a handshake were needed to seal a business deal. Shaking hands and giving one's word was considered as binding as any legal document . . . at least back in the old days.

Though the processes and procedures were different, the principle behind giving one's word and shaking hands was also binding in the ancient world. Swearing an oath or vow, or giving a pledge, was seen as a solemn promise punishable with a curse or rewarded with a blessing. In the Old Testament, oaths often took the form of "may God" do such and such (Genesis 48:20; 1 Samuel 3:17) or "far be it from me" to do such and such (Genesis 44:7, 17) or "may it be according to your word" (Exodus 8:10).

Oaths were considered sacred or profane, depending on whether or not God's name was invoked. Oaths could bind later generations, as was the case of the oath to bury Joseph in the Land of Promise (Genesis 50:24–26). Oaths could be unconditional or conditional. And oaths could be taken to declare one's innocence of a crime.

Genesis 24:2 and 47:29 mention the strange practice of placing a hand under the thigh of another person while swearing an oath. Because of the proximity of the thigh to the male reproductive organ, this practice probably carried with it the idea of swearing on one's life or one's good family name. This was particularly poignant in both references because Abraham and Jacob (Israel) were near death. The oath Abraham's servant made was conditional since Abraham didn't know whether the servant would find a wife for Isaac or whether the woman would be willing to marry Isaac (24:8). On the other hand, Joseph's oath to bury his father in the Promised Land was unconditional and binding (47:29).

Related passages: Genesis 21:31; 38:17–18; Joshua 24:16; 2 Samuel 21:17; Nehemiah 5:12; Matthew 5:33–37

25:31–34 Birthrights and Blessings

The Hebrews practiced the law of primogeniture—the special and exclusive privilege of inheritance granted to the eldest son. This practice, as noted in Scripture, was known as "the birthright" and was typically established for the firstborn son of a legal wife or a concubine.

The birthright, which was passed from father to eldest son—though the father could confer it on any son of his choosing—carried with it significant responsibilities and rewards, including:

- A double portion of the father's inheritance
- Precedence over his brothers as head of the family
- The duty to mentor younger brothers in the family
- The responsibility as the protector of widows and unmarried daughters in the family

The giving of the birthright was often, though not always, accompanied by a blessing—the invocation of God's favor upon the firstborn male and his descendants. In the Old Testament, blessings communicated spiritual, physical, and prophetic truths. Sometimes blessings were given after the birthright was conferred and often also were pronounced upon sons who had not received the birthright.

Birthrights were forfeited by committing serious sins and could be traded among brothers, as was the case of Jacob and Esau.

Related passages: Genesis 49:1–27; Deuteronomy 21:17; 1 Chronicles 5:1

28:18–22 Pillars of Remembrance

God is a remembering God. And the Hebrews were a remembering people. Throughout the long history of Israel, the people developed traditions to help them remember their identity as God's chosen people. Even today, orthodox Jewish men wear prayer shawls and phylacteries (little boxes containing Scripture worn on the forehead and hand) to help them recall God's Word and remind them of God's activities among His people.

But before these traditions of worship and remembrance, the ancient Hebrews remembered God's presence or significant events in their lives by setting up pillars. Jacob set up a memorial or sacred pillar to commemorate God's visiting Jacob in his dream. We often think of pillars as columns supporting a roof, but this was not the case of Jacob's pillar at Bethel.

Standing stones at Tel Gezer

Ancient pillars could be anywhere from simple and short to elaborate and tall. In Jacob's case, the pillar was a simple stone, anointed with oil. However, the childless Absalom may have erected a decorative pillar to commemorate his name (2 Samuel 18:18).

In addition to being used to memorialize God's presence or activities or to remember the life of individuals, pillars were used to commemorate peace treaties or covenants between former enemies, as was the case with Jacob and Laban (Genesis 31:43–53).

Related passages: Genesis 35:14, 20; Exodus 24:4; Joshua 24:26–27; 1 Samuel 10:2

39:1   An Ancient Secret Service

Protective details or bodyguards are not a modern invention. From ancient times, kings and queens employed men whose job was personal protection. Potiphar, the master of Joseph, was the Egyptian "captain of the [Pharaoh's] bodyguard" (Genesis 39:1).

Outside of the Bible, little is known of Potiphar or his title. Genesis 39:1 designates him as an "officer of Pharaoh," meaning he was a high-ranking advisor to the unnamed Pharaoh. Potiphar's specific responsibility as a royal advisor was to oversee the bodyguard. This very well could have included heading up the protective detail for Pharaoh, but it for sure entailed commanding the royal prison—the very same prison Joseph was thrown into when he was falsely accused of attacking Potiphar's wife (Genesis 39:20; 40:3).

Related passages: 2 Kings 25:8; Jeremiah 52:14

43:32   Wash Up before Dinner

"Wash your hands before you eat." This admonishment didn't originate with modern-day moms; ancient Egyptian moms probably said something very much like it. Egyptians were known to be a fastidious people, often bathing daily and adhering to strict dietary customs. For example, Egyptians held cows as sacred—their goddess Isis had the body of a woman and the horns of a cow—and therefore would not eat beef. They would not use foreign cooking utensils for fear that such utensils might have prepared a meal of beef. Nor would they kiss a non-Egyptian, such as a Greek, because that non-Egyptian might have eaten beef for supper.

Image of Egyptian cow

Egyptian dietary customs also applied to sheep. Egyptians detested shepherds (Genesis 46:34) and would not eat the flesh of sheep—a staple in the Hebrew diet (Deuteronomy 14:4). Egyptians viewed themselves as racially and religiously superior to their foreign neighbors. Therefore, they "could not eat bread with the Hebrews, for that is loathsome to the Egyptians" (Genesis 43:32). It's no surprise, then, that when Joseph hosted a meal for his Hebrew brothers, he seated them at a separate table from the Egyptians.

Related passage: Exodus 8:26

50:2−3, 26　Bring Out Your Dead

Death was an intimate fact of life in the ancient world. And how various cultures dealt with the dead was also intimate and imbued with meaning. The Greeks and Romans cremated their dead. The Hebrews buried their dead either in the ground or in caves. Though preparation and burial of the body were generally made in haste, funerals

A sarcophagus

could be elaborate. But the Egyptians practiced the most elaborate and intimate burial rite of them all.

Egyptians buried their dead, but only after the body was embalmed. The purpose of embalming was to preserve as much of the body as possible so it might be reunited with its soul. Egyptians believed that decomposition robbed the soul of its essence, so they took great pains to halt that process.

Embalming might take up to forty days and involved the removal of most of the vital organs—the heart, the lungs, and the liver, which were dehydrated and placed into ceremonial jars—while the body itself was mummified. The brain was removed through the nose and replaced with a resinous paste to fill the cranial cavity. The body was then entwined with linen treated with a mixture of salt, spices, and gums. After bandaging, the body was placed in a papyrus carton painted with religious symbols. Wealthy Egyptians and nobles might be placed within three different coffins, the last being a decoratively carved stone sarcophagus.

Egyptian law prescribed seventy-two days of mourning for deceased pharaohs. Scripture tells us the Egyptians mourned Jacob for seventy days (Genesis 50:3). This period of mourning included the forty days of embalming.

And though Jesus wasn't embalmed, His body was wrapped in spiced linen as a means of anointing, according to Jewish practice.

Related passages: Genesis 50:25; Exodus 13:19; Joshua 24:32; Mark 16:1; John 19:39 – 40

EXODUS

1:11 Enslaved in Egypt

By the time of the Exodus, the Hebrew people had lived in Egypt for centuries. They began their sojourn in the country when Joseph was sold by his brothers to a group of Midianite traders. The Midianites took him on their travels into Egypt, where they sold him to the captain of Pharaoh's bodyguard (Genesis 37:28, 36). In this case, slavery took the form of one individual buying another. Like many other nations of that era, Egypt involved itself in a robust slave trade fed primarily by the purchase or capture of foreigners.

Joseph was eventually released and honored in Egypt, and his immediate family lived there in peace and prosperity. But the Hebrew people ultimately fell under the dominion of a ruler who did not know the long-dead Joseph. The Hebrews were then placed under another type of slavery. Rather than individual ownership, the Egyptian people subdued the Hebrews as a people group, subjecting them to forced labor (Exodus 1:11). After the Hebrews' release from their Egyptian captors, the Lord compared their enslaved condition to life as a working animal. In vivid and unmistakable terms, God reminded the Hebrews of how He had ended their dehumanizing state (Leviticus 26:13).The Bible also explicitly recognizes other forms of slavery for their dehumanizing qualities (Genesis 27:40; 1 Kings 12:4; Isaiah 47:6).

Related passages: Deuteronomy 5:6; Micah 6:4

2:3   Baskets as Boats

The basket used by Moses's mother to ferry the young boy down the Nile River was made of rushes that grew on the riverside. These strong, hollow, grass-like plants were weaved together to form baskets. With some

river mud to seal them, these baskets could be converted into small floating vessels. The Hebrew word used to describe Moses's basket, *tebah*, is the same word used to describe Noah's ark. Just as Noah was saved through water, so, too, was his descendant Moses.

Similar types of baskets made of rushes, palm branches, willow branches, and even large leaves existed in the ancient Near East.

Image of Moses afloat in a reed basket

Some baskets were large and strong enough to carry heavy objects such as stone and clay, while others were smaller and used to carry fruit, meat, and freshly harvested crops.

Related passages: Deuteronomy 26:2; Judges 6:19

5:7   Brick Building

Bricks in the Old Testament era were primarily of the sun-dried variety. The brick maker would add water to the dirt and then mix the combination with a hoe, creating a thick and gooey mud. He then deposited the mud into wooden brick molds to fashion the mud into bricks right on the ground. Then, lifting the mold, he left the brick to dry in the sun. Brick makers would create rows and rows of such bricks, which, once dried and hardened, could be used to build walls and buildings. Brick kilns were much less common in the Old Testament era than the New, though we read of them occasionally (2 Samuel 12:31). Bricks were especially common in areas that lacked significant stone resources, as the latter were preferred when available.

But what about the Egyptians forcing the Hebrews to make bricks without straw? Where does straw fit into the brickmaking process? Brick makers required straw when there was either too much or not enough clay in the ground. With too much clay, the straw served to keep the bricks from cracking in the hot sun. With too little clay, the straw served to hold the mud together. Therefore, when the Hebrews were forced to make bricks without straw, they were faced with the likelihood of not meeting their quotas due to bricks falling apart, either early or late in the process, depending on the quality of the ground in their particular location.

Mud bricks

Related passages: Genesis 11:3; Nahum 3:14

7:11 Hocus Pocus

Magicians and sorcerers are mentioned occasionally in Scripture, always negatively (Deuteronomy 18:10; Jeremiah 27:9). While magic was accepted in some ancient cultures (such as that of the Egyptians), Jews and Christians considered sorcerers and magicians among those who would be judged by God (Malachi 3:5; Revelation 21:8; 22:15). *Magic* and *sorcery* refer to individuals harnessing supernatural powers outside themselves, often in the realm of the demonic. Since the practice of magic and sorcery was prohibited for Jews and Christians, people who participated in these secret arts were excluded from their communities. In fact, magicians occupied such a negative place in the thinking of Christians that Simon Magus—the magician the apostles encountered in Acts 8:9–24—became the figurehead for all heretical teaching in the first few centuries of the church.

Related passages: Daniel 2:2; Acts 13:8

12:1–13   Rescued from Tragedy

The traditional Passover meal finds its roots in God's rescue of His people from bondage in Egypt. Nine plagues had failed to convince Pharaoh to let the Hebrews go free. God's people could avoid the tenth plague—the death of all the firstborn sons and livestock—if they followed God's specific commands. Those commands included sacrificing a lamb at twilight, spreading the lamb's blood on the doorposts of the home, roasting the lamb whole over a fire, eating bitter herbs and unleavened bread with the meal, and consuming the meal while dressed to leave at a moment's notice (Exodus 12:3–11).

The Passover Feast seems to have been celebrated throughout Jewish biblical history, if not regularly, then at least during times of faithfulness and obedience. Joshua led a celebration just as the people entered the Promised Land (Joshua 5:10–12), while certain faithful kings are also recorded as having celebrated the feast (2 Chronicles 30:1–27; 35:1–19). The traditional Passover celebration at the temple continued into the New Testament era until the Romans destroyed the temple in AD 70. By New Testament times, several elements had been added to the traditional celebration, including the consumption of four cups of wine. Participants drank these four cups at certain times during the meal, and the cups symbolized God's redeeming work, based on the verbs in Exodus 6:6–7: the Cup of Sanctification ("I will bring you out from under the burdens"), the Cup of Deliverance ("I will deliver you"), the Cup of Redemption ("I will also redeem you"), and the Cup of Praise ("I will take you for My people"). When Jesus drank from the cup at the Last Supper—itself a Passover meal—many scholars believe He commented as He drank from the third cup, the Cup of Redemption (Matthew 26:27). The Passover meal is still practiced to this day.

Related passages: Exodus 34:25; Ezra 6:19–22; 1 Corinthians 5:7

12:14–20   Rejoicing Over the Exodus

God decreed that the seven-day Feast of Unleavened Bread was to begin the day after the Passover Feast. By the time of the New Testament, the two feasts had become a single, eight-day celebration (Matthew 26:17).

When the Hebrews left Egypt, they had to do so quickly while the Egyptians were still reeling from the effects of the tenth plague. To make bread with yeast would have required time for the bread to rise; it was time that the Hebrews didn't have, as they left the only homes they had ever known for the Promised Land. Celebrating the Feast of Unleavened Bread served as a reminder of that fast dash to freedom. During the eight days of the feast, no leavening agent was allowed in the house, nor was anyone allowed to eat anything with leaven in it (Exodus 12:19).

Unleavened bread

Israel's feasts were also often connected with agricultural markers. The Feast of Unleavened Bread corresponded with the beginning of the barley harvest. Therefore, a tradition developed in which, on the first day of the feast, a priest would wave a sheaf of ripened barley to consecrate the harvest. Such a tradition draws a powerful connection between the rescue from Egypt and the material blessing of the Promised Land.

Related passages: 2 Chronicles 30:13; Ezra 6:22

16:16; 29:40; 36:9   Measuring Up

When God gave direction to His people, He operated within the bounds of what they understood. One of the ways the Old Testament illustrates that principle is through units of measurement, which all the people would have been familiar with.

These units of measurement were also significant for the community, as some people would try to swindle others by using improper measurements. In the Old Testament, the most common units of length and volume (with the standard in each category appearing first) were as follows:

Length

- Cubit (Exodus 36:9): Anywhere from 18 to 21 inches or, more roughly defined, the length of a man's outstretched arm from the elbow to the tip of the middle finger

- Span (28:16): About a half-cubit or 9 to 11 inches

Volume

- Ephah (16:36): 40 liters

- Omer (16:16): 4 liters

- Homer/Kor (Ezekiel 45:14): 400 liters

- Bath (45:11): 37 liters

- Hin (Exodus 29:40): 370 liters

Related passages: Leviticus 19:36; Proverbs 20:10

20:8–11   A Day for Rest

The seventh day of the week—what we in the modern world call Saturday—was officially appointed by God for rest and special worship when He delivered the Ten Commandments (Exodus 20:8–11). God's people had observed something like this Sabbath day before receiving the Ten Commandments (16:23), but only after the Commandments did they observe it as a specific and regular practice. Moses's giving of the Decalogue connects the practice of the Sabbath to an imitation of God in creation. The Lord created for six days and rested on the seventh;

therefore, His people were to work for six days and rest on the seventh. The Israelite priests were to sacrifice an extra lamb at the temple on the Sabbath as well (Numbers 28:9). In the New Testament, Jesus affirmed His lordship over the Sabbath while acknowledging there should be a humanitarian aspect to the observance (Mark 2:23–28). Believers see in the Sabbath a spiritual rest that comes as a result of the indwelling Holy Spirit and also look forward to a future time of rest that will not only be spiritual but material as well (Hebrews 4:9).

A shofar announces the beginning of the Sabbath.

Related passages: John 9:16; Colossians 2:16

23:16   Celebrating God's Provision

The Feast of the Harvest, or Feast of Weeks, was a one-day festival celebrating the end of the barley harvest. During this festival, the people were to make an offering of the first fruits from the harvest, bringing two loaves of bread along with seven lambs, a bullock, and two rams (Leviticus 23:15–18). God wanted the Feast of Weeks to be a celebration that included the entire community—not just the free Jews but also their male and female servants, the priests, and the widows, orphans, and foreigners among them (Deuteronomy 16:10–11). God intended for the feast to be a time for the people to remember His faithful provision for them.

The Feast of Weeks took on added significance in the New Testament era, as it was on this day that the new Christians in Jerusalem first received the Holy Spirit (Acts 2:1–4). The Greek name, *Pentecost*, means "fiftieth day," referring to the number of days after Passover that this feast begins.

Related passages: Exodus 34:22; Numbers 28:26–31

23:16   Remembering the Wandering Years

Due to their disobedience, the Israelites wandered in the wilderness for forty years before entering the Promised Land. During that time, they lived in small, portable buildings called booths or tabernacles. The Feast of Booths (or Tabernacles) called the people to look back on that time of wandering by building and living in small structures for seven days (Leviticus 23:40–43). The feast is also called the Feast of the Ingathering due to its timing, which came at the end of the general harvest season around October. The priest offered seventy bullocks during the festival—along with two rams, fourteen lambs, and a sin offering of one male goat each day (Numbers 29:12–34). Every seventh year, during which there was no harvest, the Mosaic Law was read to all people in the towns, including children and even foreigners (Deuteronomy 31:9–13). The Israelites celebrated the Feast of Booths under Ezra upon their return to the land (Ezra 3:4), while the prophet Zechariah pictured the festival as annually drawing people of all nations to Jerusalem during the millennial kingdom (Zechariah 14:16–19).

Related passages: Matthew 17:4; John 7:2

28:1–43   Dressed to Bless

The high priests dressed differently from the rest of the population of Israel, with clothing that set them apart for the sacred work of the priesthood. They wore their unique clothing during their time of service but dressed normally while "off duty." The priestly garments, which covered the head and the whole body, were fashioned with cloth of multiple colors and decorated with many precious stones.

- Ephod (Exodus 28:6–14): The ephod was an apron-like garment worn over the priest's robe, draping down to about the knees. Two shoulder pieces were joined to the body of the ephod. On top of each shoulder piece was a stone of onyx engraved with the names of the twelve tribes, six on each stone. The two shoulder pieces were connected to the breastpiece with "chains" of woven gold thread.

- Breastpiece (Exodus 28:15–30): The breastpiece, in the shape of a square, attached to the front of the ephod on the priest's chest. The breastpiece was made of multicolored cloth like the ephod and lined with four rows of precious stones—three in each row. The stones were all different in both type and color, signifying the twelve tribes of Israel. Further, the ephod and the breastpiece were attached with blue thread at the bottom of the breastpiece to keep the breastpiece in place. The

Image of priestly garments

breastpiece was fitted with a pouch which held the Urim and the Thummim—an unknown means of revelation used by the high priest to discern God's will.

- Robe (28:31–35): Underneath the ephod, the priest wore a blue robe, lined around the neck with woven threadwork to prevent tearing. Around the hem of the robe hung multicolored, woven pomegranates and golden bells. The bells could be heard tinkling whenever the priest walked.

- Turban (28:36–39): On the priest's head, he wore a linen turban with a plate of pure gold attached to the front of it. On the gold plate, the words "Holy to the LORD" were engraved in Hebrew. This stated in the clearest of terms the position of the priest as he made offerings on behalf of the people.

- Tunic (28:39): The priest wore this garment, woven from fine linen, as an undergarment beneath the robe, ephod, and breast-piece. On Yom Kippur, the Day of Atonement, the high priest entered the Holy of Holies dressed in only a special linen tunic, linen turban, and sash (which were worn only once), leaving the other priestly garments behind (Leviticus 16:4).

- Sash (Exodus 28:39): The priestly vestments were completed with a linen, multicolored sash tied around the outside of the ephod (39:29).

Related passage: Exodus 39:1–31

40:17–33   Outfitting the Worship Space

The tabernacle—also called the Tent of Meeting—served as the portable worship space for the people of Israel. They originally built the tabernacle during their time of wandering in the Sinai Desert after their release from bondage in Egypt. It served the people until Solomon constructed the temple in Jerusalem more than four hundred years later. The tabernacle itself was a tent separated into two rooms (the Holy Place and the Holy of Holies), surrounded by an outer courtyard that contained the altar of burnt offering. The construction of the tabernacle involved the crafting of several pieces that would aid the priests in their service at this place of worship.

A modern-day replica of the tabernacle in Timna Park, Israel

•   Curtains and Framework (Exodus 40:17–19): The curtains of the tabernacle were sewn together from fine linens dyed with blue, purple, and scarlet. Images of cherubim were woven into them, creating fine tapestries for the walls and ceiling of the tabernacle. A frame built of gold-covered acacia wood served as a support (26:15–30), and a curtain of goats' hair was placed over the tapestries to protect them from the elements (26:1–14).

•   The Ark of the Covenant (40:20–21): The ark of the covenant was a small box of acacia wood covered in pure gold. Stretching just short of four feet across and just over two feet deep and wide, the box was affixed with four small feet at its base to keep it from resting directly on the ground. Attached to each foot was a gold ring to accommodate two long poles, so that the ark could be transported without being touched. Atop the ark was a slab of pure gold, with two gold cherubim attached to the ends (25:10–22). Moses placed into the ark the stone tablets upon

which God wrote the Ten Commandments (Deuteronomy 10:5).
A jar of manna and Aaron's staff were also kept in the ark
(Exodus 16:34; Numbers 17:10; Hebrews 9:4).

- Veil (Exodus 40:21): A veil separated the Holy of Holies, which
  contained the ark of the covenant, from the Holy Place. Like the
  outer curtains, the veil was made of blue, purple, and scarlet
  material and fine twisted linen, ornamented with embroidered
  cherubim, and hung with hooks from four pillars of acacia wood
  (26:31–35).

- The Table of Showbread (40:22–23): The table of showbread, or
  the table of the bread of the Presence, was three feet long, eighteen
  inches deep, just over two feet high, made of acacia wood, and
  overlaid with gold. God's people were also instructed to fashion
  dishes of pure gold to hold the bread as it sat on the table or
  other offerings to be made (25:23–30; Leviticus 24:5–9).

- Lampstand (Exodus 40:24–25): Made of pure gold, the lampstand had six branches, three on each side, attached to a central
  trunk. With bulbs on the end of each branch and at the top
  of the trunk, totaling seven in number, the lampstand took on
  the appearance of a tree. The lampstand sat inside the Holy
  Place, lighting an area that included the table of the bread of the
  Presence (25:31–40).

- Altar of Incense (40:26–27): The altar of incense sat just outside
  the Holy of Holies. The altar was a square table three feet high,
  made of acacia wood, and overlaid with gold. The table had four
  horns coming up from its corners, upon which Aaron would
  place the blood of the sin offering every year on the Day of
  Atonement. The altar's main function was to continually display
  burning incense before the Lord. Aaron was to change it every
  morning and every evening when he trimmed the wicks of the
  lampstand (30:1–11).

- Screen (40:28): In front of the main entrance to the Holy Place
  was a screen made of blue, purple, and scarlet material and fine

twisted linen, hanging with hooks from five pillars of acacia wood (Exodus 26:36–37).

- Altar of Burnt Offering (40:29): Made of acacia wood overlaid with bronze, the altar of burnt offering was seven and a half feet square and four and a half feet tall and was located in front of the tent of meeting. The altar had four horns, one at each corner, as well as a bronze grating halfway down, covering the entire altar. Underneath the grating the priests could start fires to roast the offerings, which were laid upon the grating itself. The people were also to fashion pails, shovels, basins, and fire pans to clean out the area under and around the altar (27:1–8).

- Laver (40:30–32): The laver, or basin, sat just beyond the altar of burnt offering and before the Tent of Meeting itself. The priests filled this bronze structure with water and used it to perform ritual washings before entering the Tent of Meeting (30:17–21).

- Courtyard (40:33): The courtyard was an open area around the Tent of Meeting, bounded on its edges by pillars of acacia wood and hangings of fine linens. The courtyard was 150 feet long and 75 feet wide, with an entrance that faced east. Israelite men and women could enter the courtyard with their personal offerings, as long as the individuals were clean according to the Law (27:9–19).

Related passages: 1 Chronicles 6:32; Hebrews 9

LEVITICUS

—❦—

1:3–17   Offering Offerings

If the ancient Israelites are known for anything, they're known for having been a religious people. The center of their lives revolved around the worship of Yahweh. And the center of Yahweh worship revolved around sacrificial offerings. The book of Leviticus was the handbook for how the children of Israel were to offer sacrifices to Yahweh and to live holy lives.

The offertory system of ancient Israel could be complex, but generally, three different types of offerings existed:

Offerings of Consecration

Consecratory offerings emphasized the surrender of the worshiper to God.

- Burnt offerings (Leviticus 1:3–17) were the most frequent sacrifices in Israel because of their close association with sacred seasons in the Hebrew calendar. The burnt sacrifices of bulls, sheep or goats, and birds were prescribed as continual, daily offerings and signified *complete* acceptance by God of the worshiper.

- Grain or cereal offerings (2:1–16) usually consisted of a mixture of baked fine flour, olive oil, and frankincense. Grain offerings normally accompanied burnt offerings as an indication of commitment and gratitude to God for the forgiveness represented in the burnt offering.

Offerings of Community

Communal offerings were voluntary, except during the Feast of Booths (Leviticus 23:19–20) and in the case of one who took a Nazirite vow (Numbers 6:17–20). Communal offerings were made on behalf of the entire people. The most basic communal offering was the peace offering (Leviticus 3:1–17), which followed the same basic prescription of burnt offerings. However, certain portions of the peace offering were allotted to the priests for food. Peace offerings included:

- Wave offerings (Leviticus 7:30–34)
- Thanksgiving offerings (22:29)
- Votive offerings (Numbers 6:17–20)
- Ordination offerings (Leviticus 8:22–32)

Offerings of Cleansing

Cleansing or purification offerings were sacrifices made for violations of God's Law and were intended to represent the worshiper's repentance of sin.

- Sin offerings (Leviticus 4:1–35) prescribed different types of animals depending on the rank or wealth of the offender. By placing his or her hand on the animal while it was sacrificed, the offender identified with the need for a blood sacrifice to bring about cleansing. The priest collected the blood and smeared it on the horns of the altar and then the animal was burnt according to the Law.

- Guilt offerings (5:1–19) were specialized kinds of sin offerings, which involved atoning for transgressions against someone else. For every kind of guilt offering, the offender had to confess his or her sin, make full restitution plus a fine of one fifth in the case of objects being harmed, and make a sacrifice.

Related passages: Exodus 29:19–34; Leviticus 6:8–18, 24–30; 7:1–21; 8:27, 29; 9:21; Numbers 15:22–29

8:23–24   The Priests' Bloody Ears

Priestly work was bloody. All day, every day, priests handled sacrificial animals . . . and that meant handling blood. But before a man could do the duty of a priest, he had to be ordained into the priesthood . . . and that also was bloody work.

At the ordination of Aaron and his sons, Moses sacrificed a ram and smeared some of the ram's blood on the right earlobes, right thumbs, and right big toes of Aaron and Aaron's sons. This anointing with blood signified that Aaron and his sons were consecrated to the service of God—that they were completely devoted to the Lord, from head to toe. But the symbolism goes further. The right side signified the place of divine honor and power. Aaron and his sons stood as God's representatives before the people. And as they performed their priestly duties before the Lord, they were to listen to God's voice (earlobe), to work diligently in God's service (thumb), and to faithfully follow and obey God's leading (big toe).

High priest with Pentateuch scrolls

While the practice of placing blood on the earlobe, thumb, and big toe was primarily associated with the ordination of priests, it was also prescribed for cleansed lepers. In the case of a healed leper, the practice signified only the removal of guilt and acceptance back into the community of faith (Leviticus 14:14).

Related passage: Exodus 29:20–21

13:1–59   Rash and Removal

Few diseases struck with more terror in the ancient world than leprosy. In Israel, those who carried the disease were ostracized from the community of faith.

The definition of leprosy in Scripture applied to the destructive disease of the skin, nerve endings, and bones. It included, but did not necessarily apply exclusively to, our modern-day notion of leprosy (Hansen's disease). Other skin diseases or welts were also deemed leprous, including swellings, scabs, and bright spots (Leviticus 13:2), infections (13:6), white and raw patches (13:10), and scaly infections in the scalp (13:30).

The leper was considered ceremonially unclean and was, therefore, isolated from the community for observation. Though leprosy was not necessarily a result of sin, the root of the word *leprosy* means "to strike," which led the ancient Israelites to believe that God had stigmatized lepers. Therefore, leprosy became an enduring illustration for sin.

We tend to think of leprosy as only a skin condition, but the disease could transfer to the leper's garments as well (13:45 – 59). Regardless of where the condition was located, only priests could pronounce a leper clean, at which point the leper made a guilt offering and was marked by blood on the right earlobe, right thumb, and right big toe (14:14).

Related passages: Psalm 51:7; Isaiah 1:6; Luke 17:11 – 19

16:2, 13 – 15   Lord, Have Mercy

Every person has a natural desire to know and worship the divine. So wrote Solomon in Ecclesiastes 3:11.

Since the dawn of human history, we've longed to see the face of God. Moses asked permission to see God's face — His glory — and was told: "You cannot see My face, for no man can see Me and live!" (Exodus 33:20).

Other ancient worshipers carved idols from wood, stone, and metal in an effort to capture images of their gods, believing that the idols embodied the gods' very presence.

But no idol can capture Yahweh's image or His glory. And no building can contain His presence (1 Kings 8:27). But because of God's great mercy, He chose to make His dwelling among His people, Israel. And, in the days of their wilderness wanderings, the place of God's presence was the mercy seat. Just as God's presence manifested itself in the pillar of cloud by day and the pillar of fire at night, so God's glory resided as a cloud between the outstretched wings of the carved cherubim sitting atop the ark of the covenant, which was located in the Holy of Holies section of the tabernacle.

A replica of the ark of the covenant

It was there, before the mercy seat, that the high priest sprinkled sacrificial blood for the sins of the people on the Day of Atonement, praying that God would show mercy to Israel and forgive the nation's sins.

Related passages: Exodus 25:17–22; Leviticus 16:1–4; Hebrews 9:3–7

16:8–10 An Escaped Goat

Individual sins become national sins when a people and their rulers are stubbornly persistent in disobeying God. Every nation—ancient and modern—has demonstrated disregard for the seriousness of their sins. However, very few people these days think about the sins of their nation. Our focus is often more personal and private. This would have been true of ancient Israel as well, if not for the specific ritual God graciously provided to remove the stain of shame and condemnation from the nation of His chosen people.

On the Day of Atonement, the priest selected two goats—one to be sacrificed to the Lord as a sin offering and the other to serve as Israel's symbolic proxy of national atonement, the scapegoat.

The Hebrew word for "scapegoat," *azazel*, is difficult to interpret. According to rabbinic tradition, the *azazel* represented a place where the goat was sent. Others view *azazel* as the name of a demon living in the wilderness who was believed to consume the goat and thereby consume the nation's sins. But the demonic idea would be out of place for a people destined to be wholly dedicated to God.

Regardless of the exact meaning of the word *azazel*, the significance of the scapegoat was its symbolism. As the scapegoat was released into the wilderness, it symbolized the transfer of guilt and the removal of sin from the nation. Their sin and guilt were gone forever, never to return.

Related passages: Leviticus 16:26; Psalm 103:12

18:21; 20:2–5 Passing through the Fire

"Thou shalt not let any of thy seed pass through the fire to Molech." This is how the King James version translates Leviticus 18:21.

Image of the statue of Molech

From the very beginning of Israel's history, God prohibited idol worship, and few idolatrous practices were as detestable as sacrificing to the Ammonite god Molech (also known as Milcom). According to rabbinic writers, idols of Molech featured a human form with an ox's head. Constructed of bronze, these statues were hollow and placed over a fire to heat them within.

Worship of Molech involved human sacrifice . . . child sacrifice. The record of the precise practice of Molech worship is sketchy, but it is assumed that children (possibly while still alive) were either placed within the statue, which acted as a furnace, or cast into the open flames beneath the statute. Rabbinic tradition held that the children were immolated inside the idol while the priests of Molech beat drums to drown out the death cries.

As hard as it is to comprehend, at different points in their history, the Israelites erected Molech idols and engaged in the practice of passing their children through the fires. For those who did, God's prescribed punishment was severe: they were to be stoned to death.

Related passages: Deuteronomy 12:31; 2 Kings 23:10; Jeremiah 32:35

20:14; 24:14–16   Under Sentence of Death

In Genesis 9:5–6, God laid the foundation of government and established the first human law: capital punishment. The basis for the law was the *Imago Dei*—the fact that humanity is made in the image of God. To destroy or degrade another person is to destroy or degrade the character of God manifested in that individual—an affront to the very God in whose image all humans are made.

At the time the Israelites received an expanded treatment of God's Law in Leviticus, capital punishment broadened as a consequence not only for murder but also for adultery, incest, idolatry, blasphemy, violating the Sabbath, disobeying the Word of God, priestly daughters committing fornication, and rebellion against parents. The Lord didn't prescribe the means of execution in Genesis 9, but in Leviticus, Numbers, and Deuteronomy (the books of the Law) He prescribed three methods.

- Stoning: This common mode of execution required at least two witnesses to substantiate a charge, and the witnesses had to throw the first stones.

- Burning: This was an unusual mode of execution, reserved for cases of incest (Leviticus 20:14) and harlotry by a daughter of a priest (21:9).

- Impaling: This was the usual mode of execution, using a sword, for communities that had committed apostasy (Exodus 32:1, 27) or idolatry (Deuteronomy 13:12–15). This method could be used by the "blood avenger" against those who had committed murder (Numbers 35:19–21).

Related passages: Genesis 38:24; Leviticus 20:2, 27; 24:23; Numbers 15:32–36; Deuteronomy 13:1–5; 17:2–7; 21:18–21; 22:22–23; Joshua 7:25

25:1–7   A Year of Rest

God isn't a workaholic. And He doesn't want any of His children to be one either. This is why the Lord commanded the Israelites to observe a day of rest every seventh day (Exodus 20:8–10). What most people don't know, and what the Israelites soon forgot, is that God didn't want the land He had given His people to be worked beyond its means to support an abundance of crops.

The Lord commanded that every seventh year—the sabbatical year—the land of Israel was to lie fallow and be allowed to grow naturally, without cultivation. What grew in the untended fields and vineyards would be harvested as provisions for all the people, regardless of ownership. The sabbatical year reminded the Israelites of three important truths. First, it demonstrated that the land, like all creation, was under the sovereign rule of God, not humanity. Second, it strengthened the people's faith in the Lord, the real provider of all that's needed for life and happiness. Third, by making every person of equal status for the year, it reminded the people to care for the poor during the unequal years of sowing and reaping.

The sabbatical year was an enduring command. If the people ever disobeyed God's Word, He would remove them from the land for a time (Leviticus 26:34–35, 43). So when the Israelites deprived the land of seventy sabbaths over a 490-year span, God kept His Word, resulting in the people's seventy-year captivity in Babylon (2 Chronicles 36:20–21).

Related passages: Exodus 23:10–11; Jeremiah 25:8–12; Daniel 9:1–2

25:8–34   A Year of Celebration

God is the champion of liberty—and not just spiritual liberty. When He gave the children of Israel the Promised Land, He intended for them to own property and cultivate it for themselves and their posterity. But through the circumstances of life, some people fell into poverty and had to either sell their land or themselves into indentured servitude to pay off their debts.

However, because it was never God's desire for His people to be in bondage or deprived of the gift of land, He provided a means for the release of those in servitude and a means of reclamation for those who sold their land. On the tenth day of the seventh month (the Day of Atonement), after a lapse of seven sabbatical years (every forty-nine years), the people were to blow a trumpet announcing the fiftieth year as the Year of Jubilee.

During this year of celebration, liberty was proclaimed throughout the land (Leviticus 25:10). The poor Israelites who had hired themselves out were released to return to their own land debt-free (25:39–41; Deuteronomy 15:1–2). Land that had been sold since the previous Jubilee was restored to the hereditary family that originally owned it, according to the fixed title assigned by God. Because the Jubilee Year excluded the possibility of selling land permanently (Leviticus 25:23),

Green spice crops in modern-day Israel

when land was sold, prices became fixed proportionally based on the number of crops remaining until the next Jubilee, ensuring equity (25:15–17, 25–28).

Related passages: Numbers 36:4; Judges 3:11; Ezekiel 46:17

NUMBERS

1:1–3 Population Counts

The book of Numbers opens with a census and later records a second counting of the people. The census was used often in the ancient world, especially to determine those eligible for taxation and military service. In Numbers, both censuses counted only the males of Israel and were used to determine how many able-bodied men could fight in their army (Numbers 1:2–3; 26:2–3). The second census was also used to determine the particular inheritance that each family would receive once they entered the Promised Land (26:53–56).

Exodus 30:12 records the first census in Israel's history, as the Lord instructed Moses to count every adult for the purposes of collecting a tax to build the tabernacle. David's census in 2 Samuel 24 was considered sinful because David conducted the count on his own, rather than at God's command, choosing to trust in his military might rather than God's power.

Related passages: 1 Chronicles 21:1; 2 Chronicles 2:17

4:6 Covered with a Porpoise

When the tabernacle was set up, the Israelites needed a strong, durable covering for the fine tapestries that served as the walls of the worship space. They also needed to protect the ark of the covenant while they traveled. God answered these needs by directing the people to use porpoise skins (Exodus 26:14; Numbers 4:6). However, having received these instructions while in the midst of the Sinai Peninsula, where would they have acquired porpoise skins?

Dugong

To narrow down an answer to this question, we first need to look at the word itself. The rare Hebrew word translated "porpoise" in the NASB is also translated "badger" (NKJV) and "goatskin" (ESV). However, the use of the same word in Ezekiel 16:10 implies a material of great value and thereby rarity—which wouldn't apply to badger or goat skins. The translation "sea cows" (NIV) comes nearest to "porpoise" and is probably most accurate. The Gulf of Aqaba, along the eastern edge of the Sinai Peninsula, has historically contained a population of dugongs, a type of sea mammal with a porpoise-like tail. The 8- to 10-foot skins of the dugong would have been especially useful in stitching together the large outer covering of the tabernacle. Further, in the ancient world, the dugong was caught more frequently, as porpoises proved more elusive.

Related passages: Exodus 39:34; Numbers 4:14

6:1–21 Set Apart for God

Making a special commitment to one's deity was a common practice in the ancient Near East. As they did so, individuals would take upon themselves certain regulations and practices that would easily distinguish them from others in their community. Among Israelites, these dedicated people were called Nazirites. When undertaking the Nazirite vow, an individual would abstain from wine and grapes, refrain from cutting his or her hair, and avoid contact with corpses (Numbers 6:1–8). By following these special practices, the Nazirites acknowledged their devotion to God. This not only enhanced their personal pursuit of God but also stood as a living witness of faithfulness to their communities. Nazirites could end their vows by making offerings at the temple and shaving their heads. While the Nazirite vow was normally a personal choice to express one's devotion, the most well-known biblical Nazirites were Samson and Samuel, who were both Nazirites from birth (Judges 13:7; 1 Samuel 1:22). The practice of taking Nazirite vows continued into the New Testament era, with John the Baptizer being the most famous Nazirite in the days of Jesus (Luke 1:15). Beyond the New Testament era, Christian monks imitated the practice of the Nazirites, engaging in certain practices to their own spiritual benefit, as well as to the benefit of their communities.

Related passages: Acts 18:18; 21:23–26

8:4   If I Had a Hammer

In the ancient world, having the proper tools was vital. From setting up a living space to fashioning other tools and decorations, people used hammers for a wide variety of purposes. Ancient hammers were made from shaped stones outfitted with a bored hole for a handle. Such hammers would have been used to shape precious metals in the production of the tabernacle (Numbers 8:4), drive tent pegs into the ground or through enemies (Judges 4:21), or for stonemasonry (Jeremiah 23:29). Larger stone hammers were used for the purposes of war (51:20).

Related passages: Isaiah 41:7; Jeremiah 50:23

Ancient hammer

14:6 Torn in Two

The tearing of one's clothes was a common sign of mourning in the ancient Near East. Overcome with grief over a death or a destructive choice, the rending of garments offered an outward sign of an inward feeling. The Bible records numerous instances of individuals tearing their clothes for all manner of troubles. Reuben tore his clothes when he returned to find his brother Joseph sold into slavery (Genesis 37:29). Joshua tore his clothes during the conquest after the Israelites were defeated at the city of Ai (Joshua 7:6). And David tore his clothes when he heard about the death of Israel's king Saul (2 Samuel 1:11). Poor choices, crushing defeats, and the death of Israel's (fallen) leader—each of these circumstances drove people to this expression of overwhelming sadness.

Related passages: 1 Kings 21:27; Acts 14:14

18:21 Tithing One's Treasure

The Hebrew word translated "tithe" in Numbers 18:21 and elsewhere in the Old Testament can also be translated "tenth," thus explaining the connection between tithing and ten percent. Tithing is a practice almost as old as the earliest stories of the Bible. The practice appeared first in the days of Abraham when, after a military victory, the Patriarch gave a tithe to the priest/king of Salem, Melchizedek. The practice of tithing was codified in the Mosaic Law, as the Israelites were called to give to God a tenth of their flocks and their harvests (Leviticus 27:30–32). They offered the tithe before they enjoyed the fruits of their labors, signifying their gratitude for the harvest as a gift of God. The recipients of the tithe—the priests—used the offerings as sustenance, as the tribe of Levi (from which the priests came) did not have the inheritance in the Promised Land that the other tribes had (Numbers 18:20–23). Later, Israel's kings exacted a separate tithe by decree, as Samuel had warned would happen (1 Samuel 8:15–17), while Israel's propensity to turn from God led to the tithe being discontinued at certain times (Malachi 3:7–12). The New Testament carries no specific command to offer a tithe, focusing instead on cheerful giving (2 Corinthians 9:7).

Related passages: Deuteronomy 26:1–15; Amos 4:4

19:6   Lined with Cedar

Growing as tall as 120 feet, the stately cedar tree described in Scripture was found primarily in Lebanon, north of Israel. Its durability and appealing fragrance made it popular for a variety of uses. In Scripture, we see cedar used in the construction of David's palace (2 Samuel 5:11) and Solomon's temple (1 Kings 6:9) and in idol-making (Isaiah 44:13–14). The people used cedar in special circumstances, testifying to the need

to import it when used in large quantities—as for building. Solomon engaged Hiram, king of Tyre, to cut and export the cedar needed for the temple. To get the timber to Israel, Hiram brought the freshly cut trees to the sea and transported them south by way of rafts specially constructed for the purpose of carry-

Lebanon cedars

ing trees (1 Kings 5:6–10). Cedar was used only rarely in the Israelite's ritual worship—for example, in pronouncing clean the healed leper (Leviticus 14:4) and in sacrificing the red heifer for purification (Numbers 19:6).

Related passages: Judges 9:15; Psalm 92:12

21:13   The Arnon Border

In ancient times, much like today, rivers and other natural markers often served as borders between nations. The Arnon River was one such significant border, serving as the dividing line between the Moabites to the south and the Amorites to the north. Later, the Arnon River served as the southern border of the lands east of the Jordan River which were granted to Reuben, Gad, and the half-tribe of Manasseh. The Arnon River pours into the Dead Sea near the sea's midpoint and begins some 45 miles to the east. Other prominent natural borders in the Bible are the Jordan River, which served as Israel's eastern border, and the Litani River, which served as the border in the northwest corner of Israel.

Related passages: Numbers 22:36; Jeremiah 48:20

22:41   Worshiping Baal

Baal was the Canaanite fertility god. The culture of worship around this god served as a thorn in the side of the Israelites almost from the time they occupied the Promised Land. This god was associated with storms and fertility, the rain creating a fertile environment for crops and livestock to flourish. Baal would, therefore, sometimes be associated with images such as lightning (storms) and bulls (fertility). The people of Canaan believed Baal to have power over the weather to varying degrees, based on Baal's encounters with the god of death, Mot. As the prophets of Baal told stories of their god's victories or defeats, so the people believed the weather would turn favorable or unfavorable.

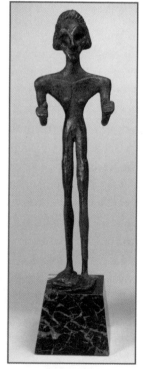

The first biblical image of Baal worship occurs in Numbers 22:41, where the biblical text pictures Balaam at special places devoted to Baal in Moab, Israel's neighboring community.

Image of male votive figure of Baal, early second millennium BC

The people of Israel fell into Baal worship to varying degrees during their time in the Promised Land, as evidenced by temples to Baal in Samaria and Jerusalem (1 Kings 16:32; 2 Kings 11:18). Baal also became the subject of a significant event in the Old Testament, as the prophet Elijah challenged Baal worship under Israel's King Ahab by setting up an altar to God to compete with an altar devoted to Baal. God blessed Elijah's act miraculously, showing Himself to be in power over all of heaven and earth (1 Kings 18:20–39).

Related passages: Jeremiah 2:23; Zephaniah 1:4

27:1–11   No Inheritance for Women?

All inheritance in biblical Israel was tied back to the people's original inheritance of the land from God, when Joshua led them in conquering the Promised Land. At the time of the conquest, each tribe received certain sections of the land to be divvied up by families within that tribe. Historically, when the leaders of those families died, their estates—which focused first on their land—reverted to their sons. However, some families had no sons, only daughters. In many cultures, that would have meant a transfer of land to the uncle or male cousin of those daughters. But in Israel, the Mosaic Law made special provision for women in these circumstances to ensure that the land stayed within their families (Numbers 27:7–8). The only condition for receiving the inheritance was that the women were to marry men within the tribe of their father, so that the land would remain within the tribe of their birth (36:6).

Related passages: Numbers 36:8; Job 42:15

DEUTERONOMY

11:18 Wearing God's Word

God told the Israelites to teach His commandments so that the younger generation, who did not witness the plagues in Egypt or the wilderness miracles, would know, worship, and obey Him. God described the principle by which His people should teach His Law to the next generation—by binding it on their hands and wearing it as a frontal on their foreheads. But what did this mean?

Frontals, also known as frontlets, were a common form of decorative headdress worn in ancient Syria and Israel.[1] Possibly as early as the third century BC, some Jews started creating phylacteries—small, black boxes that held Scripture—to be worn on the forehead and left arm. Jews wrote the words of Exodus 13:9, 16 and Deuteronomy 6:8; 11:18 on pieces of parchment and put them in the boxes. Some Jews wore phylacteries to show their commitment to God's Word, but others may have had a superstitious motivation. Many people at this time, pagan and otherwise, attached special protective powers to religious objects.

Many Jews took God's command literally, but He wanted them to ingrain His Law into their minds and obey Him with their actions. God didn't intend His Word to act as an amulet or a good luck charm; He wanted His people to know His Word and live it out. God requires obedience that flows from a mind fixed on His Word and deeds inspired by love for Him.

Related passages: Matthew 4:1–4; John 14:15–26

11:20   Decorative Doorposts

Before He delivered them from slavery in Egypt, God commanded the Israelites to slaughter a lamb and brush its blood on the doorframes of their houses. When the angel of death saw the blood covering their doors, he passed over them (Exodus 12:1–29). The Israelites displayed this symbol of God's grace on their doorframes and continued to commemorate that event each year at Passover. Passover identified the Israelites with God and served as a reminder of God's mercy to His people.

Ancient doors were often made of wood and had a threshold, vertical side pieces (doorposts), and a supporting upper beam (lintel). Egyptian doors had metal sockets on which the doors opened and closed, but Israelite doors often had stone sockets. God's people applied Deuteronomy 11:20 literally and decorated their doorposts with God's Word.[2]

Gates stood prominently on the ancient roads and welcomed travelers into a city. Gates had two wooden halves decorated with metal and wooden nails. Business, government, legal proceedings, and social meetings took place at the city gates. While God didn't necessarily want His people to scribble His Law on their gates, He did intend for their obedience to His Law to be obvious to others who entered their cities and their lives. God intended His Word to guide the Israelites as they carried out legal, governmental, and personal business. In this sense, therefore, the Lord wanted His people to write His Law on their gates.

Related passages: Deuteronomy 6:5–9

11:29   Speak from the Mountains

Mount Ebal and Mount Gerizim stand on opposite sides of the Shechem pass in the hills of Samaria. These two mountains stand approximately 3,000 feet above sea level, but Mount Ebal is 230 feet higher.[3] Moses commanded the Levites to read the curses from Mount Ebal and the blessings from Mount Gerizim (Deuteronomy 27:12–13). He instructed half of the tribes to stand on Mount Ebal and the other half to stand on

Mount Gerizim. Their proximity, with a valley in between, allowed the Israelites to hear the reading of the blessings and curses.

The town of Shechem held a strategic location between Mount Gerizim and Mount Ebal, at the crossroads of two main highways. In Genesis 12:6, Abram entered the land God promised to give to the patriarch's descendants by way of Mount Gerizim and Shechem. In Genesis 33:18–20, Jacob entered the future Promised Land, bought a plot of ground, and settled near Shechem. Later, after Joshua and the nation had taken control of their new land, he gathered them at Shechem for rededication to the Lord (Joshua 24:1–28). Shechem remained a significant place for the Israelites even after the kingdom split and the focus of power shifted to Jerusalem under King David.[4]

Mount Ebal

God chose these two mountains as the location for reading the blessings and curses because they reminded the Israelites of God's promise to give them a land and a future (Genesis 12:1–4). Both mountains are in the northern part of the land God promised to the Israelites.

Related passage: Joshua 8:30–35

12:13–14   The Place of Sacrifice

When the Israelites settled in their new home, they were surrounded by cultic places of worship. The Canaanites had set up altars to false gods on high places, on hills, and under trees. God commanded His people to destroy all the Canaanites' idolatrous places of worship when they conquered their land (Numbers 33:52). God demanded the Israelites' hearts, souls, minds, and worship.

Canaanite altar at Megiddo (foreground)

In Deuteronomy 12:13–14, Moses instructed God's people not to sacrifice their offerings in just any religious spot they came across. Because the pagans worshiped their gods "on the high mountains and on the hills and under every green tree," God would designate a specific place for worship, and there was to be no alternative.

God designated the place of worship to be first at Shiloh, after which David brought the ark of the covenant to Jerusalem, where Solomon would build God's temple (Joshua 18:1; 2 Samuel 6:17; 1 Kings 6:1). God's presence in the tabernacle and, later, the temple made them holy. Because God alone deserved His people's devotion, He established a specific place of worship so the Israelites wouldn't fall to the false religions of their neighbors.

Related passage: 1 Kings 3:1–3

14:1–3, 21; 22:5, 9–11   Be Distinct!

The Israelites lived among many nations who worshiped many gods. God wanted His people to remain holy and distinct from the pagans. So God set standards for the Israelites to follow that would distinguish them from other nations. Deuteronomy lists a number of these standards.

- Deuteronomy 14:1: God commanded His people not to cut themselves nor shave their foreheads for the sake of the dead. The Canaanites included cutting and shaving in their mourning rituals (Leviticus 19:27–28 and 1 Kings 18:28). The Israelites tore their clothes, wore sackcloth, and sprinkled dust on their heads when they grieved for the dead, but they did not participate in the Canaanite rituals.

- Deuteronomy 14:3: God prohibited His people from eating detestable foods. The distinction between the holy and the profane, the clean and the unclean, set Israel apart from the other nations. Pagans didn't make these distinctions, so Israel's unique laws and worship made them obviously different—holy unto the Lord. Some of the prohibited animals played a part in Canaanite religions.

- Deuteronomy 14:21: God told His people not to eat anything that died on its own. If an Israelite found an animal that had died on its own, it most likely had not been drained of blood in the way prescribed by God. Because eating blood was practiced in pagan religions at that time, God didn't allow His people to eat animals—even clean animals—if their blood had not been removed. But they could give the animal to a resident alien or sell it to foreigners.

- Deuteronomy 14:21: This passage includes a strange prohibition not to boil a young goat in its mother's milk. This odd command prevented Israelites from participating in a fertility ritual common in the Canaanite and Syrian religions.[5] Ancient Near Eastern peoples were agricultural and relied on consistent rain for crop production and healthy animals. They believed the Canaanite storm god, Baal, controlled the rain and rivers.[6] These people conducted many rituals to provoke their gods to provide rain and fertility. Because a mother's milk symbolized health and fruitfulness, these pagans sought the gods' help with the harvest by boiling a goat in its mother's milk.

- Deuteronomy 22:5: God also forbade men and women from wearing each other's clothing. So what was the big deal about cross-dressing? This practice may have been part of Canaanite religion and culture and was most likely linked with homosexuality. Regardless, God created male and female with inherent differences to jointly bear His image. To overturn His created order would imply a lack of faith in His wisdom, sovereignty, and role as Creator and Ruler.

- Deuteronomy 22:9–11: God commanded the Israelites not to wear mixed fabrics, unequally yoke animals, or sow mixed seeds. These prohibitions don't seem to indicate a practice among Israel's pagan neighbors, but most likely these rules underscored God's command that the children of Israel live as His holy, separate people. Just as they weren't to mix worship of the one true God with idolatry or mix morality with immorality, they were to keep fabrics, seeds, and animals separate. It was cruel to yoke different animals together to plow the field. God cares about the animals He created, and He expects His people to care about them too.[7]

Related passages: Leviticus 11:45; 19:2; 20:7–8; 1 Peter 1:15–16

19:14   Stealing Land

In biblical times, property was received by lot and inheritance. Owning property in the ancient world created an atmosphere of financial equality and allowed each family to provide for its own needs, as well as the needs of the poor. Property ownership also reminded the Israelites that God had given them the imperative to steward the land He created. Taking care of their property evidenced God's image in His people.

Moses prepared God's people for their entrance into the Promised Land by commanding them not to move an ancient boundary stone that demarcated the tribes' inheritances (Deuteronomy 19:14).

A boundary stone at Gezer, Israel

God established those borders, and to move one of the stones was tantamount to stealing divinely given land. Ultimately, theft revealed a lack of faith in and respect for God's sovereignty.

Deuteronomy 32 records Moses's song that taught the Israelites about God's character and His actions on their behalf. In Deuteronomy 32:8, Moses reminded the Israelites that God had established the boundaries of the nations. Not only did God exercise control over Israel, but He ruled over all people. The tribes of Israel, therefore, were to respect the limits of their territories and allow each tribe to enjoy the land given them by God.

Related passages: Deuteronomy 27:17; Proverbs 22:28; 23:10

20:5–8   Honorable Discharge

Today, soldiers who desert their branch of the military may face criminal charges. But in ancient Israel, members of God's army were permitted to leave their service under certain circumstances. A man who had recently built a house but hadn't yet lived in it could go home and experience the fruit of his labor. And if a man had just planted a vineyard but hadn't yet benefited from his crop, he could go home to enjoy his bounty. The engaged man could leave the military in order to marry and spend time with his new wife. And finally, the fearful man, who may not have trusted in God's sovereignty in war, could turn back so he wouldn't discourage his fellow soldiers.

God wanted total commitment and faith among His warriors. If any soldier had a divided heart and longed for home, he risked distracting the other men from fighting hard and trusting God.[8] God cared about both the morale of His army and the desires of His people.

Related passages: Judges 7:3; 1 Corinthians 9:7

25:4 Benefits of Hard Labor

Deuteronomy 25:4 says: "You shall not muzzle the ox while he is threshing." The verse doesn't include an explanation, but we can determine its meaning from the historical context.

In biblical times, cattle represented wealth—more cattle meant more riches. People used cattle for farming, meat, milk, clothing, and sacrificial purposes. Farmers used oxen to plow fields and thresh grain.[9] Threshing grain consisted of separating wheat from chaff on the threshing floor using a sledge with sharp stones underneath, pulled by a team of oxen.[10]

Oxen

Oxen surely built up an appetite doing the hard work of threshing. When the hungry beasts started to eat the valuable wheat, farmers would put muzzles over their mouths so they wouldn't devour all the grain. In Deuteronomy 25:4, God prohibited this practice. If He wanted oxen to receive sustenance and benefit from their hard work, how much more the servant of God (1 Corinthians 9:9–10)?

Related passage: Proverbs 12:10

31:26–28 Holy Witnesses

Witnesses testify to the truth or inaccuracy of a claim. When a modern-day judge convicts someone of a capital crime, the conviction often relies on the testimony of witnesses, DNA evidence, or both. In the Bible, any offense deserving death required at least two eyewitnesses—and these witnesses had to be so sure of their testimony that they would cast the first stone to kill the convict (Deuteronomy 17:5–7).

In Hebrew, the word *edut* means "testimony" and refers to the tablets on which God wrote the Ten Commandments. As a result, the Bible refers to the ark of the covenant, which held the tablets, as the "ark of the testimony" (Exodus 25:22). When Aaron placed his budding rod outside the Tent of Meeting as evidence of God's sovereignty, the tent became the Tent of the Testimony (Numbers 17:7–8). And the curtain separating the innermost room in God's house from the common areas, which served as a witness of His holiness, was called the veil of testimony (Leviticus 24:3).[11] These physical reminders—these witnesses—testified to God's holy character, intimate care, and religious expectations for the Israelites.

Witnesses played a crucial role in the ancient Near East. In non-Israelite covenant ceremonies, written agreements between equals or between conquering kings and vassal kings ended with a list of witnesses to the treaty. The conquering king's gods served as the most prominent and important witnesses to the covenant. Parts of nature also witnessed the treaty, including heaven, earth, mountains, seas, and rivers.[12] In Deuteronomy 31:28, Moses called heaven and earth as witnesses to the Israelites' obedience or disobedience to God's Law.

Related passages: Joshua 22:26–28; 2 Corinthians 13:1

JOSHUA

—❦—

2:1 Ancient Espionage

The Bible records the use of spies in warfare. In Deuteronomy 1:22–25, Moses sent twelve representatives, one from each of the tribes, on a reconnaissance mission to check out the Promised Land. In Judges 18:1–10, five spies explored Laish as the tribe of Dan sought to move north. And in Joshua 2:1, two scouts entered Jericho as the army of Israel prepared to attack the walled city.

When the spies arrived in Jericho, they met Rahab the harlot. She hid them on her roof and, to protect them, lied to her own government. Deception played a crucial part in wartime espionage. In hiding the scouts, Rahab committed treason.

Joshua's strategy in dispatching these spies coincided with the war strategy of the ancient Near East at that time. Israel's neighbors used espionage as a tool during war to assess an enemy's defenses and to determine whether to invade another country. When Joshua sent the spies, they looked for crucial information about Jericho, including its strengths and weaknesses.

Related passage: Numbers 13

2:15 Tight Quarters

Rahab lived within the wall of Jericho, so her home provided an ideal hiding place for the Hebrew spies. Ancient Near Eastern city walls consisted of two walls with perpendicular supports. The thicker, stronger outer wall, together with the inner wall, provided protection for the city.

To make efficient use of the space between the walls, people built homes there.[1]

Wall homes resembled modern townhouses and were either attached to the city walls or to adjacent homes. The ancients plastered the interiors of the walls and made floors of clay (for modest homes) or flagstone (for more extravagant dwellings).

These homes had two stories. The first floor was used for cooking, sleeping, and housing animals. It had a low ceiling—about six feet high—and wood doors that opened and closed on wooden doorframes with sockets.[2] The second, rooftop level had a flat floor on which residents would arrange and dry flax and other fibers (Joshua 2:6). They built the rooftop level with reed matting covered with thick clay and buttressed by wood columns.[3]

Related passage: 2 Samuel 11:2

A mud brick wall in Jericho

3:6   Priests in Ancient Warfare

In the ancient Near East, war and religion went together like peanut butter and jelly. Many nations fought and conquered in order to uphold the honor of their patron gods—even though these false gods remained aloof to the peoples' conflicts and problems.

A pagan king was the human counterpart to his nation's god. Devotees believed that the warrior gods (Baal/Hadad, Marduk, and Re) defeated the chaos powers (Yamm and Leviathan) in the war that resulted in the creation of the earth and people. Worshipers believed pagan kings were to subdue their enemies in order to maintain order and increase power.[4] As long as pagan kings "created" their kingdoms by winning wars, they acted as worthy counterparts to their gods. And, because war was an inherently religious undertaking, pagan kings used priests to incite the warrior gods to come to their aid.[5] The pagan priests played an important role in warfare, using black magic and curses to get the false gods to act on their behalf.

Unlike the gods of the nations surrounding the Israelites, Yahweh was not a "national" God. He would reign supreme above all gods and idols, regardless of whether Israel won or lost a battle (Isaiah 45:5–7). Yet, He also cared intimately about His people and involved Himself in their actions.

The Israelites, as God's chosen people, prayed for the Lord's help and often worshiped Him in preparation for war (1 Samuel 7:8–10). The Israelite priests played a central role in warfare of their nation. They carried onto the battlefield the ark of the covenant, which represented God's presence. When Israel marched against an enemy, the priests reminded them not to fear and encouraged them to trust in God's protection. They recalled God's promises and Moses's words: "Do not be afraid of [the enemy], for the LORD your God will personally fight for you" (Deuteronomy 3:22 NET).

Related passage: Ephesians 6:10–17

3:10   The Who-ites?

The book of Joshua records the Israelites' journey to their new home. Regrettably, other peoples had already taken up residence in this land. So, as a part of the Israelites occupancy, they had to defeat and displace seven nations. But who were these people?

- **Canaanites:** According to Numbers 13:29, the Canaanites lived in the Jordan Valley and in the lowlands near the sea coast.[6] Genesis 10:19 records the boundaries of Canaan: "And the territory of the Canaanite extended from Sidon as you go toward Gerar, as far as Gaza; as you go toward Sodom and Gomorrah and Admah and Zeboiim, as far as Lasha." But the Amarna Letters—ancient correspondence between Egyptian and Canaanite rulers—refer to the entire Phoenecian coast as "the land of Canaan."[7]

  Approximately thirty city-states and rulers comprised Canaan, according to the records in Joshua 12:7–24. Joshua led Israel into this land in four stages, and the first strategic city they conquered was Jericho. Canaan had an agricultural economy, but its inhabitants were also known to be merchants. The word *Canaanite* can be translated "merchant."

The Canaanites had advanced arts, sciences, and technology. They built walled cities superior to the construction methods of the Israelites and produced ceramics, musical instruments, and architecture. When Solomon built God's temple, he employed Phoenecian (Canaanite) artisans (1 Kings 7:13–51) and used their artistic patterns and designs.

In addition to cultural refinement and technological savvy, the Canaanites contributed an elaborate, pantheistic religion to the ancient Near East. In stark contrast to Israel's monotheistic worship of Yahweh, the Canaanites worshiped the gods El (the cruel ruler of the gods) and his son Baal (the bull-god of thunder), as well as the goddesses of fertility and war, Anath, Astarte, and Ashera. Canaanites also bowed to secondary gods: Mot (god of death), Reshep (god of pestilence), Shulman (god of health), and Koshar (god of the arts).[8]

- **Hittites:** The center of the powerful Hittite kingdom covered eastern, central Anatolia (modern-day Turkey). The Hittite kingdom probably extended into Syria, to the border of Palestine, or beyond. In fact, the residents of Luz built a city in the Hittite territory (Judges 1:26). The Hittites mentioned in the Bible prob ably traveled south and intermingled with the Israelites.

  Many Hittites appear in the Bible and were among some of the groups that the Israelites didn't completely destroy. Uriah, King David's loyal soldier, was a Hittite (2 Samuel 11:3–6). Hittites numbered among King Solomon's forced laborers (1 Kings 9:20–21). And several Hittite women were in King Solomon's harem (11:1).[9]

- **Hivites:** The Hivites lived in the northern part of Canaan, near Tyre, "at the foot of Hermon in the land of Mizpeh" (Joshua 11:3). According to Genesis 34:2–31, the Hivites focused on trade and increasing their flocks and herds, and they avoided warfare. They worshiped Baal-berith, which means "Baal of the coalition." Even their idol of choice preferred peace.[10]

As evidence of their peaceful disposition and their crafty diplomacy, the Hivites living in Gibeon lied to Joshua and pretended to live in a faraway land (Joshua 9:3–15). They established a covenant with Joshua because they heard about the Israelites' violent destruction of Jericho. The Hivites would rather have served the Israelites than to have gone to war against them.

- **Perizzites:** The Perizzites inhabited Canaan and lived in the hill country of Ephraim, part of the central highlands (Joshua 17:15–18). Not much about their identity is known. They may have lived in unwalled towns, as the word *Perizzite* may come from the word *paruz*, which means "a dweller in an unwalled village." [11]

- **Girgashites:** The Girgashites descended from Canaan, son of Ham, son of Noah, just like the rest of the tribes on this list—except the Perizzites—(Genesis 10:15–16). The Girgashites lived in the land of Canaan, west of the Jordan (Joshua 24:11). Not much else is known about them. [12]

- **Amorites:** The Amorites lived in the Transjordan area of Canaan, including the territory of King Sihon at Heshbon and King Og at Ashtaroth and Edrei. Israel defeated these kingdoms under Joshua's leadership, as recorded in Deuteronomy 2–3. The Amorites spoke a language similar to Hebrew and worshiped idols. [13]

- **Jebusites:** The Jebusites lived in the hill country and didn't shy away from conflict. Even though Joshua defeated the king of Jebus, the Jebusites retained some control of Jebus until the time of King David. Second Samuel 5:6–8 records King David's occupation of Jebus,

Ruins at the City of David, the site of ancient Jebus

which then became Jerusalem. Only King David's expert military skill could dislodge the Jebusites from this fortified city with thick walls and a strategic position on a hill between the Kidron, Tyropoeon, and Zedek valleys.[14]

Related passage: Deuteronomy 7:1–6

5:2 Making the Cut

Flint is a type of quartz that flakes into sharp fragments when struck with a hard object. For this reason, this sharp stone served as a knife in the ancient Near East. Flint could be found in Syria, Israel, and Egypt. It

also developed within chalk or limestone in northern Samaria, western Galilee, and in the Jordan Rift Valley.[15]

Flint dominated as the early material of choice for tools and knives. In time, iron,

Flint knife

bronze, and copper took the place of flint, but the Israelites continued to use flint knives in the rite of circumcision (Joshua 5:2–3).

Flint was so hard that several prophets used it to powerfully illustrate spiritual truths. The prophet Isaiah spoke of the Lord's promised Servant and His unflinching determination in the face of persecution:

> For the Lord God helps Me,
> Therefore, I am not disgraced;
> Therefore, I have set My face like flint,
> And I know that I shall not be ashamed. (Isaiah 50:7)

The prophet Zechariah used flint to illustrate the hardness of the Israelites' hearts and their unwillingness to obey God's Word (Zechariah 7:12).

Related passages: Exodus 4:25; Deuteronomy 8:15; Ezekiel 3:9

6:1–5 Strategies of War[16]

The Israelite army organized into groups of ten, fifty, one hundred, and one thousand men, led by captains (2 Samuel 18:1; 2 Kings 1:9; 2 Chronicles 25:5). The soldiers divided into three groups: the front, middle, and rear guard (Joshua 6:9). On occasion, God directed the army to wait for the enemy and surround them from behind (2 Samuel 5:23–25). And sometimes, one hero from each side dueled instead of both armies engaging in battle (1 Samuel 17).

Israel's enemies may have had expert soldiers and walled cities. When attacking a fortified city, it was common practice for ancient Near Eastern armies to perform a siege, which involved camping next to the target city, cutting off access to roads and water, and going over, under, or through the city walls. For example, Egyptian armies would set up ladders to scale fortified city walls or use battering rams (metal-tipped, wooden beams carried by soldiers under a protective covering) to break through the city gate.[17] God instructed His people to perform a most unusual siege on Jericho, one that left no room for human credit.

Though it seemed the Israelites were the underdogs, God gave them victory. Even when their enemies were equipped with armored chariots (Joshua 17:16–18), Joshua's army burned those chariots and hamstrung the horses (11:6).

Later, King Solomon improved Israel's military prowess by setting up fortified cities in which he stored armaments. Israelite chariots had three riders—a driver, a warrior, and a shield-bearer—while Egyptian chariots carried only two men—a driver and a warrior.

Related passages: Exodus 14:13–31; 2 Kings 19:32–37

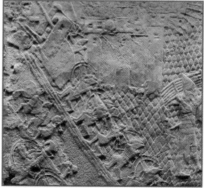

Image of Assyrian battering ram from the reliefs of the Lachish siege

8:18   Battle Tools

Spears and javelins represented different forms of the same weapon. All of Israel's neighbors used these weapons in warfare. Spears were used by the Sumerians around the fourth millennium BC and even earlier by hunters to kill animals. First made from a sharp blade attached to a stick, spears were used throughout the ancient Near East to defend cities against attack—especially when invaders used ladders to climb over city walls.[18]

Spears were longer and heavier than javelins. Egyptian double-edged spears, made of wood, ranged from five to six feet long and had a bronze or iron head. Spears used by the Assyrian infantry were shorter than the men that used them, but those used by the cavalry were longer, like the Egyptian spears.

Javelins looked like spears but were small enough to throw at enemy troops. The Mesopotamians and Egyptians used javelins beginning in 2500 BC. And by the fourteenth century BC, the Egyptians kept several quivers full of javelins on every chariot.[19]

King Saul most likely threw a heavy spear at David in 1 Samuel 18:10–11. And the giant Goliath used a large, heavy spear when fighting against young David in 1 Samuel 17:7.[20]

Related passages: Joshua 8:26;
Job 41:26–29

Replicas of ancient spears

8:31   Building Altars

Following the victory over Ai, the road was clear for Israel to make their way to Mount Ebal and Mount Gerizim. There, Joshua constructed an altar of uncut stones, just as Moses had commanded. God prohibited elevated altars with stairs, made of hewn stone (Exodus 20:22–26). But why?

In the biblical era, Israelite and pagan altars consisted of raised stone or earth, with a flat top, usually where priests sacrificed animal offerings. Ancient pagans believed that their gods lived in the large stones used to make altars and that the blood of sacrificed animals would strengthen their gods. Canaanite altars had steps, and as the priests ascended, their feet and legs were exposed. God didn't want His holy priests to bare their feet and legs during a solemn, sacrificial ceremony.[21]

Pagan altars sometimes had images and names of false gods carved on them.[22] This may have explained why the Lord commanded the Israelites not to use carved or ornamented stones in their altars. God wanted to separate His people from their heathen neighbors and prevent them from confusing worship of the one, true God with worship of false deities.

Related passage: Exodus 27:1–7

10:12–13   The Book of Jashar

Joshua 10:12–13 records the day when the sun and moon stood still so that God's people, under Joshua's leadership, could defeat the Amorites. Originally written in Hebrew, the book of Jashar records this event as follows:

> And when they were smiting, the day was declining toward evening, and Joshua said in the sight of all the people, "Sun, stand thou still upon Gibeon, and thou moon in the valley of Ajalon, until the nation shall have

revenged itself upon its enemies." And the Lord hearkened to the voice of Joshua, and the sun stood still in the midst of the heavens, and it stood still six and thirty moments, and the moon also stood still and hastened not to go down a whole day. And there was no day like that, before it or after it, that the Lord hearkened to the voice of a man, for the Lord fought for Israel. (The Book of Jashar 88:63–65)[23]

But what was the book of Jashar? Joshua 10:13 and 2 Samuel 1:18 both mention this mysterious volume. Although no known copies of the book of Jashar exist today, it must have existed at some time since the Bible refers to it. The book apparently recorded some events in Israel's history. Most likely written in poetry, this document gained the respect of those who lived at the time it was written.[24]

Experts can't determine the origin of the book of Jashar, but it may have resulted from a gradual collection of historical writings. Instead of chronicling Israel's official, national past, the book may have been a compilation of songs with historical import.[25]

The Hebrew word *jashar* means "upright." So this book may have recorded the works of upright individuals or of the nation as a whole, which was viewed as the only upright nation among the pagan peoples of the ancient Near East.[26]

JUDGES

2:9 Where to Bury?

The location of burial sites in the Old Testament era varied, depending on the time period and the social status of the deceased individual. Those with little money, travelers, or nomadic people were usually buried in shallow graves covered with stones, the heft of the rocks preventing wild animals from disturbing the freshly buried bodies. Often the sites chosen were easily marked and remembered, such as under a tree (Genesis 35:8). Surviving family may have also erected stone pillars as markers for some graves (35:20).

Natural caves were also a common option for burial, as was the case of Abraham's family (23:19; 25:9; 50:13). As time passed in the Old Testament era, people began to carve caves from hillsides, outfitting the holes with interior shelves or niches on which they could lay bodies. They would then cover the tomb entrances with large stones.

A burial site was generally in the land of the deceased person's tribal inheritance (Judges 2:9), though most travelers were buried wherever they died. Late in the Israelite monarchy and beyond, many cities had a common grave outside the city boundaries for travelers and residents (2 Kings 23:6).

Related passages: Genesis 35:19; Numbers 20:1

2:16 Passing Judgment

Simply put, an Old Testament-era judge was a person chosen to administer justice in his or her community. The Hebrew noun translated *judge* comes from the verb "to decide." Therefore, judges were respected persons among

God's people and made decisions on issues of law or fairness. In Israel, the ultimate judge was God Himself (Genesis 15:14; Isaiah 3:13). The role of judge on earth was initially taken on within families by the elders of the family (Genesis 38:24). Any disputes or scandals involving the family were handled internally. When Israel left Egypt, Moses served for a time as judge for all the people. This unsustainable situation changed when Jethro, Moses's father-in-law, suggested adding some trusted individuals to judge alongside Israel's leader (Exodus 18:13–26).

After the conquest—during the time recorded in the book of Judges—judges achieved their roles through God's favor. In these cases, the judges rose to leadership positions in Israel so that God could use them to deal with injustice in the Promised Land. The story of Deborah indicates that her people came to her for advice (Judges 4:4–5). More than just decision makers, these judges functioned as royal or military leaders by both making decisions and carrying out actions. First Chronicles 23:4 indicates a multiplicity of judges after the kingship was established, suggesting a court system administered by a select group of Levites.

Israel and Judah's refusal to follow God faithfully led to the prophetic criticism of many of the nations' practices, including the corruption of their judges (Zephaniah 3:1–3).

Related passages: Hosea 13:10; Zechariah 8:16

3:3 Goliath's People

The Philistines were a people group settled in the southwestern portion of Canaan—later Israel—along the Mediterranean Sea. Both Abraham

The Sorek Valley was one of several that led to the land of the Philistines.

and Isaac dwelt for a time in the land of the Philistines, and the Bible records Isaac's interaction with a Philistine king (Genesis 21:31–34; 26:1–16). These early encounters with people in the land of the Philistines occurred before a great migration of people in the thirteenth and twelfth centuries BC. This migration is usually associated with the more famous Philistine encounters in Scripture, including the domination of Israel by the Philistines for short periods of time during the era of the judges (Judges 10:7; 13:1), as well as David's encounter with the most famous Philistine of all, Goliath (1 Samuel 17:1–4). In fact, most of the first half of 1 Samuel recounts battles against the Philistines as the people of Israel struggled to defend themselves against enemy incursions that stretched farther into the Promised Land. The Philistines took a much lesser role in biblical history after David's great victory over them (2 Samuel 5:25). As the Philistines' power waned, they were still a subject in the prophetic books as the Lord prepared to bring judgment upon them (Amos 1:6–8).

Related passages: Judges 14:4; Zephaniah 2:4–7

3:3   Take a Sidon

The Sidonians came from Sidon, a city on the Mediterranean Sea in the area of modern-day Lebanon, about forty miles north of the Israeli border. The ancient city of Sidon was one of the most significant settlements of the Phoenician people. Sidonians were seafaring traders as well as inventors—namely of the Phoenician alphabet, upon which modern-day alphabets are based. Sidon was a city-state, as were all Phoenician cities at that time. As a result, Sidon's inhabitants were called Sidonians, and they occupied a somewhat undetermined segment of land. City-states usually controlled the land in and around its city, but the exact boundaries varied depending on the time period and strength of the city. Sidon gained some prominence during the time of the judges, as certain extra-biblical texts use the term *Sidonians* to refer to all Phoenicians. During that period, the Sidonian lands might have extended into the northwest corner of Israel, especially along the coast. Later in history, Sidonians were well known for their timber industry (1 Kings 5:6) and for their goddess Ashtoreth—one of many influences that led King Solomon astray (11:5).

Related passages: Joshua 13:6; Ezekiel 32:30

3:13   The Aggressive Amalekites

Amalek was Esau's grandson, making the Amalekites distant cousins to the Israelites, who descended from Esau's twin brother, Jacob. The Amalekites primarily lived in the southern portions of Israel in the Negev desert. After the time of Amalek, the Amalekites' entrance onto the biblical stage came just after God brought the Israelites out of Egypt. God delivered His people from an attack by the Amalekites, as Moses stood on a hill with his hands raised (Exodus 17:8–13). This attack eventually led God to tell His people that they would "blot out the memory of Amalek from under heaven" (Deuteronomy 25:19) but not before God used the Amalekites to punish His people for their presumption when they attempted to invade the Promised Land without His blessing (Numbers 14:45). Amalek continued to be a thorn in Israel's side during the period of the judges (Judges 3:13; 6:3–5), even settling for a time in Ephraim (12:15). Both David and Saul won decisive victories against the Amalekites (1 Samuel 15:1–9; 30:1–20), leading to the Amalekites' eventual decline from the scene of history.

Related passages: 1 Samuel 15:32–33; 1 Chronicles 4:43

3:31   Staying in Line

Usually used by farmers to control large animals such as oxen, the goad, or oxgoad, was a long stick or straight branch of a strong wood carved to a point at one end. The farmer carried the goad along with him in the fields. If his animal began to drift from the furrow, the farmer used the goad to poke it back into place. The other end of the goad may have held a small metal plate, used to scrape accumulated dirt from the plow. We see evidence of this other end of the goad, or "hoe," in 1 Samuel 13:20, which suggests that the Philistines needed to sharpen the goads, a process accomplished by a blacksmith. Ironically, the judge Shamgar used an oxgoad to kill six hundred Philistines.

Related passages: Ecclesiastes 12:11; Acts 26:14

4:7   Down by the River

The Kishon River was the site of two significant conflicts in Old Testament history. This river, which begins in central Israel, flows northwest past Megiddo and out into the Mediterranean Sea. Farmland throughout the wide and fertile Jezreel Valley receives its water from the Kishon. This area of flat and open land played a pivotal role in the

Israelites' defeat of Jabin, king of Canaan, and his chief lieutenant, Sisera. While twenty thousand Israelites under the judge Deborah and military leader Barak gathered on the isolated hill of Mount Tabor just north of the Kishon River, Sisera and his nine hundred chariots approached from the river to the south. When Barak attacked at Deborah's command, Sisera and his army of chariots turned back across the plain. The soft ground near the Kishon slowed the chariots enough for Barak's Israelite army to catch them and win the victory.

Kishon River

Related passages: 1 Kings 18:40; Psalm 83:9

6:2   Caught in the Midian

The Harod Valley, site of Gideon's victory over the Midianites

The nation of Midian was located to the southeast of Israel, probably as far south as the Gulf of Aqaba. Midian's complex history in relation to God's people began with the birth of a child, Midian, to Abraham's second wife, Keturah (Genesis 25:1–4). Not too many generations from then, Midianite traders betrayed their heritage when they purchased Abraham's great-grandson, Joseph, to sell as a slave in Egypt (37:28, 36). Many generations later, Moses left Egypt and settled with a Midianite priest named Jethro, a man whose daughter Moses eventually took as his wife (Exodus 2:15–21).

This alternation between positive and negative turned sour permanently when the Moabites and Midianites teamed up to hire Balaam to pronounce an oracle against Israel, an event which eventually led Israel to attack Midian (Numbers 31:1–9). Once Midian recovered, they badgered the Israelites until Gideon came against them with a small army and chased the Midianites out of Israel once and for all (Judges 6–8). From that time forward, Israel's victories over Midian became a significant point of encouragement that God was indeed working through His people (Psalm 83:9).

Related passages: 1 Chronicles 1:32–33; Isaiah 10:26

9:40–45   Walled In

Many cities from ancient times were built with walls surrounding them. These walls were made either of stone or of mud and bricks. Walls were generally built during times of peace in an effort to solidify a city's strength in case of an invasion from a neighboring people. The strongest cities were those walled settlements on top of hills or mountains, because a double measure of protection could dissuade attackers. Throughout much of the Old Testament period, city walls could be up to twenty-five feet thick and forty feet high. The wide tops of walls made it convenient for archers and other fighters to defend the city from an advanced position. Often, the wall widened at the base to provide support and to prevent a breach from enemy weaponry like battering rams. Because the gate represented the weakest point of the wall, entrances into cities were often well-fortified with multiple gates and even long ramps leading up to the entry.

When Abimelech came with his army against Schechem, he waited in hiding, only attacking when the Schechemites opened the gate (Judges 9:40–45). Joshua's victory at Jericho came only after the miraculous destruction of the formerly impenetrable city walls (Joshua 6:20). When Israel conquered the land, they did not immediately fortify all their cities. However, under the monarchy, fortification was emphasized (1 Kings 9:15). When Nehemiah returned to Jerusalem from exile, he, too, sought to fortify Israel's capital city by rebuilding its walls (Nehemiah 2:7–8).

Related passages: 1 Samuel 31:10; 2 Samuel 11:20

9:53 Throwing Down the Upper Millstone

If thrown hard enough, almost anything can become a weapon. In an agrarian culture where people had to grind their own grain to make bread, most households had a small mill. Usually in the shape of a rectangle, the millstone was either flat or slightly concave on top. The farmer would place his harvested grain on this flat or nearly flat surface and use an upper millstone to grind the grain. This upper millstone was often small enough to fit in a person's hand, though larger versions existed that looked something like huge,

Image of Abimelech's death from an upper millstone

stone donuts. The grinder would fit the center hole with a stick and proceed to grind the grain by rolling the circular upper millstone on top of the grain until it was ground up. When the woman attacked Abimelech, she likely grabbed the nearest heavy object that she could lift. The bulky stone, falling from a high window, would have easily killed the rogue judge (Judges 9:53).

Related passages: Job 41:24; Luke 17:2

10:6 My Name Is Aram

The Arameans occupied the land northeast of Israel, land we have known from the time of the New Testament as Syria. Aram, from whom the Old Testament nation traces its heritage, was a grandson of Noah, making the Arameans one of the most ancient people groups still in existence today (Genesis 10:22). As the biblical patriarchs came on the scene, Aram existed as several separate kingdoms, and the relationship between Israel and Aram was largely positive. Abraham sent a servant to Aram to find an Aramean wife for his son, Isaac (25:20), while Jacob also fled to Paddan-aram to find a wife (28:2). The land of Aram was held in such high esteem in this early stage that whenever the people made an offering of the first fruits of their harvests, they were to recount their history, beginning with a remembrance that their father was "a wandering Aramean" (Deuteronomy 26:5).

As time passed, the relationship between Israel and Aram soured. We see the first hints of this in the Law, when the king of Moab hired Balaam of Aram to curse Israel (Numbers 23:7). Beginning in the era of the judges, the Arameans were a more hostile force, leading the people of Israel to worship of false gods (Judges 10:6). The Arameans endured two major military losses to David's army (2 Samuel 8:5, 13; 10:1–19), and many years later, Ahab battled the Arameans often, eventually dying after being struck by an Aramean arrow (1 Kings 22:34–35). The people of Aram battled with many of the later kings of Israel and Judah (2 Kings 5–9; 12–13; 15–16), and Aram became an object of God's judgment via the prophets (Amos 1:5).

Related passages: Isaiah 17:3; Amos 9:7

10:6   A Relationship Characterized by Tension

Moab was located on a high plateau on the eastern edge of the Dead Sea between the Arnon and the Zered rivers. Lot's daughter named her son Moab, which meant "from my father"—a name that served as a constant reminder of the nation's incestuous origins. The Moabites worshiped the god Chemosh through animal sacrifice, sexual rituals, and consulting the stars. Israel was led astray by Moabite worship multiple times in its history (Judges 10:6; 1 Kings 11:33).

God's people were almost always at odds with Moab, beginning with their first encounter. After Israel conquered the Amorites, Moab joined with Midian to hire Balaam to place a curse on Israel (Numbers 22:1–6). One of the early judges, Ehud, assassinated King Eglon of Moab in order to retake Jericho and the lower Jordan River nearby (Judges 3:13, 28).

One exception to the general pattern of conflict with Moab occurs in the story of Ruth. Naomi, an Israelite, emigrated to Moab and oversaw her sons marrying Moabite women.

The Mesha Stele, or Moabite Stone, boasts of Moab's victory over Israel in ninth-century BC.

One of these women, Ruth, became the great-grandmother of David (Ruth 1:1, 4; 4:16–17). The period of monarchy saw regular conflict with Moab (1 Samuel 12:9; 2 Kings 3:1–27). David sent his own parents to Moab for their safety—which was no doubt possible because of his father's heritage—as Saul sought to kill the heir-apparent to the throne of Israel (1 Samuel 22:3–4). Like most other nations in Israel's immediate area though, Moab came under the judgment of God (Isaiah 15:1–9; Jeremiah 48).

Related passages: Psalm 60:6–8; Ezekiel 25:8–11

10:6   Distant Relatives

Located in the land to the east of the Jordan River, the Ammonites were separated from the river, first by Amorites and later by the tribes of Reuben, Gad, and Manasseh after Israel conquered the land. The people of Ammon were distant relatives of the Israelites and descendants of Lot. This relative closeness explains God's injunction that Israel was to treat the Ammonites with kindness by not attempting to conquer Ammonite land (Deuteronomy 2:19).

The citadel of Ammon in modern-day Amman, Jordan

From that high point, the history between Israel and Ammon embarked on a steady downward trajectory. Even before the Israelites entered the land, Ammon joined with Moab in hiring Balaam to deliver a curse upon Israel, thus earning a rebuke from the Lord (Deuteronomy 23:3–6). The Ammonites were active militarily against Israel during the period of the judges, while the Israelites also took on some of the Ammonites' false religions (Judges 3:13; 10:6; 11:5). After centuries of both active and passive Ammonite opposition to Israel, both Saul and David defeated Ammon (1 Samuel 11:11; 2 Samuel 10:14). Ultimately, through the prophets, God pronounced judgment on Ammon and on other hostile nations around Israel (Jeremiah 49:1–6; Ezekiel 25:1–7).

Related passages: 1 Kings 11:1; Ezekiel 21:20

10:12 A Mysterious People

Scholars know little about the Maonites—also called Meunites—who entered the biblical scene as a group that had previously oppressed the Israelites in the period of the judges (Judges 10:12). This nation, antagonistic to God's people, was likely located in a small area to the southeast of Israel. The Bible records the Maonites' presence in battle against Israel (2 Chronicles 26:7) and shows the Maonites to have kept livestock (1 Chronicles 4:41).

Related passage: 2 Chronicles 20:1

14:12 Riddle Me This

Seen as clever wordplay and often associated with wisdom, riddles were not unknown in the ancient world. Riddles make their most famous biblical appearance in the story of Samson, who made a wager of clothes with thirty Philistines if they could solve his riddle:

> "Out of the eater came something to eat,
> And out of the strong came something sweet."
> (Judges 14:14)

Some have suggested that a Hebrew synonym for "something sweet" is a homophone with the Hebrew word for "lion." This wordplay added a bit of cleverness to the riddle—as well as the key to actually solving it, as the answer is related to a personal story that was known only to Samson (14:8–9). Numbers 12:8 uses the same Hebrew root, characterizing God's speech to His prophet as "mouth to mouth," "clearly and not in riddles" (NIV). In other places, Scripture connects riddles with language for wisdom (Psalm 49:4; Proverbs 1:6). Many also liken Jesus's practice of speaking in parables to speaking in riddles, hiding the truth in plain words.

Related passages: Psalm 78:2; Ezekiel 17:2

RUTH

—❈—

1:3, 5   Woe for Widows

In the ancient days of Israel, widows, like orphans and foreigners, were to be pitied. Unless they remarried, their future often was filled with difficulties and danger. The Law allowed widows to conduct business, but because widows wore special clothing (Genesis 38:14), they became easy targets for the wicked, who often took advantage of them (Deuteronomy 24:17).

However, the Lord has always had a special place in His heart for widows, promising to be their provider and protector (Deuteronomy 10:18; Psalm 68:5). God commanded landowners not to harvest the corners of their fields, so widows, orphans, and strangers might glean the corners and thereby make bread for themselves. For those landowners who disobeyed the Lord's command or those who sought to harm widows, the Lord pronounced a curse (Deuteronomy 27:19).

Double woe belonged to Naomi and Ruth. Both were widows, and in Moab, Naomi, an Israelite, was an alien in a strange land, separated from the protection of God's Law. Ruth could have returned to her father's house, as did Orpah (Ruth 1:14–15), but instead decided to accompany Naomi to her homeland, which made Ruth the alien in a strange land. Yet, through God's grace, He provided for the two women through Boaz, their kinsman-redeemer.

Related passages: Deuteronomy 14:29; Job 24:21; Psalm 94:3–6; James 1:27

1:11–12 The Husband of My Brother's Wife

The Lord stipulated that a man could receive his deceased brother's property and manage it for his brother's widow, thereby keeping the property and possessions in the family. If the widow had no male child, the brother of the deceased was expected to take the widow in marriage (Deuteronomy 25:5). These marriages were known as *levirate*, meaning "husband's brother." Under levirate marriages, the man who had taken his brother's wife as his own was to call their firstborn son by his brother's name (25:6).

If the brother of the deceased refused to enter into a levirate marriage with his sister-in-law, she was to speak with the elders of the city who would counsel the brother. If the brother persisted in his refusal, the widow was to take his sandal and spit in his face (25:7–10).

Naomi tried to send Ruth away—back to her family—because Naomi had no other sons to marry Ruth (Ruth 1:11–12). Once Ruth decided to return with Naomi, however, a near kinsman was responsible under the levirate law to marry Ruth. When the nearest kinsman refused Ruth, another relative, Boaz, could marry her (4:1–10).

Related passages: Genesis 38:8–10; Matthew 22:24

2:2–9 Picking Up the Scraps

Jesus said, "The poor you will always have with you" (Matthew 26:11 NIV). As true as those words are today, they were just as true two thousand years ago when they were first uttered—and just as true more than a thousand years before Jesus's declaration, at the time that Naomi and Ruth immigrated to Bethlehem from Moab.

These two widowed women were poor. Both walked into Naomi's hometown empty-handed. But what they did have, they used. Naomi had family connections, and Ruth had a strong back and a humble heart. So, Naomi sent her daughter-in-law to glean in the field of their kinsman, Boaz.

Stalks of wheat

Old Testament Law prohibited landowners from harvesting the corners of their fields, from gathering fruit fallen from trees or vines, and from going back to pick missed fruit. Rather, landowners and their harvesters were to leave the corners and unpicked fruit for the poor, the orphans, the widows, and the foreigners (Leviticus 19:9–10). From these leftovers or scraps, the poor could glean their living.

Gleaning not only preserved the lives of the poor and destitute, it also taught them the value of work and prevented them from becoming an undue burden on the community.

Related passages: Leviticus 23:22; Deuteronomy 24:19–21

2:10   Falling on Your Face

God was at work in Ruth's life. Though a foreigner, she had committed herself to the worship of Yahweh (Ruth 1:16), and the Lord honored her vow. When Ruth went into Boaz's field to glean grain, Boaz promised to protect and provide for her (2:8–9). Such generosity and grace was too much for Ruth, causing her to bow before Boaz (2:10).

Bowing was a common gesture in the ancient world. It was an outward posture of an inward perspective, communicating humility, gratitude, or adoration. Bowing was practiced in the worship of God

(Genesis 17:3), in the worship of idols (Daniel 3:5–7), and in obeisance to a superior (2 Kings 4:37). While some bows consisted of dipping the head, with face and eyes cast down, and bending at the waist, the most common form of bowing was what we see in Ruth—prostration.

The biblical text says Ruth "fell on her face," but she didn't literally *fall* on her face. Rather, she probably knelt before Boaz and gradually stretched out her body until her forehead was touching the ground. And in this posture of submission, she asked why Boaz showed her such favor. His answer was gentle: because of her great respect for Naomi, her mother-in-law (Ruth 2:11). For this, Boaz blessed Ruth—a blessing the Lord honored (2:12).

Related passages: 1 Samuel 25:24–25; Matthew 26:39; Revelation 1:17

2:15–16 Bringing in the Sheaves

"Bringing in the Sheaves" is the title of an old American hymn that had significant meaning for the Christians who sang it from the late-1800s through the mid-twentieth century. But for modern-day Christians living in a culture devoid of agricultural pursuits, bringing in the sheaves has little meaning.

For Ruth and Naomi, sheaves were a matter of life and death.

Sheaves were bundles of barley or wheat that were tied together to make it easier to measure and transport the crops from the fields to

Sheaves of wheat

the threshing floor. Harvesters or reapers walked among the stalks of grain, cutting them with long, curved knives known as sickles. Trailing behind the reapers, hired gatherers—typically women—took armfuls of stalks and, with a few additional stalks, tied them together into sheaves. After the gatherers came, the gleaners then harvested any loose stalks dropped during the reaping and gathering.

When Ruth came to glean in Boaz's field, he commanded his reapers and gatherers to let her collect stalks of grain while the harvest was still being processed. But he went even further: his gatherers were to purposely "pull out" stalks of grain from the already bundled sheaves.

We see sheaves referenced throughout the Bible, such as when sheaves of barley were offered to the Lord as part of the first fruits (Leviticus 23:10–12).

Related passages: Psalm 126:6; 129:5–7; Amos 2:13

2:23 A Grain of Barley and Wheat

Naomi and Ruth arrived in Bethlehem at the right time—during harvest season in the spring (Ruth 1:22). While ancient Israelites grew and gathered many different types of fruit, only two primary grains were grown in Israel—barley and wheat.

Barley was grown and harvested mainly for animals—horses, mules, and donkeys—though it was also eaten by poor people. Sown in the fall, barley was harvested the following spring, usually in April to coincide with Passover. In the hill country, however, it was often not harvested until May or June.

Typically, four weeks after the barley harvest, the wheat harvest began, usually in late April, and continued until mid-June, coinciding with the Feast of Pentecost. Wheat was sown in winter, broadcasted widely around the field and lightly plowed into the soil. Wheat was the staple grain of Israel, grown and harvested for making bread. Wheat grew in abundance—enough to meet the needs of the people living in Israel and to export to other nations (Amos 8:5).

When Naomi and Ruth came to Bethlehem in the spring, Ruth immediately began gleaning barley in Boaz's fields. And she continued to glean through the wheat harvest. Because of her work in the fields, Ruth was able to provide for herself and her mother-in-law.

Related passages: Deuteronomy 16:9; Joshua 3:15; Luke 3:17

3:4, 7   Cold Feet, Warm Heart

It certainly seems like strange advice . . . to modern ears. But Naomi's instruction to go to the place where Boaz laid down for the night and uncover his feet made perfect sense to Ruth (Ruth 3:3–4). Some commentators see this as a brazen invitation on Ruth's part to an immoral act. They couldn't be more wrong. After Ruth uncovered Boaz's feet (3:7), he called her "a woman of [moral] excellence" (3:11).

If uncovering Boaz's feet wasn't an invitation to immorality, what did it mean to uncover his feet?

Though the practice of uncovering feet is mentioned only here in Ruth, what Naomi advised and what Ruth did apparently was a common and ceremonial practice that was completely proper. While Boaz slept, Ruth removed from his feet his outer garment, the robe he was using as a blanket, laid down, and most likely covered herself. Ruth's act was a sign of her vulnerability as a widow, but because Boaz was a near kinsman, it was also a plea for protection. And because the only way to secure Ruth's protection in the community was through marriage, uncovering Boaz's feet was an invitation—a proposal—of marriage; an invitation Boaz accepted.

Related passage: Ruth 3:8–13

3:13   The Goal of a *Gaal*

Ancient Hebrew families were tightly knit together, rarely living apart in separate villages. If a stranger came into a town, such as Bethlehem, where Naomi, Ruth, and Boaz lived, he or she would quickly discover that family units included extended family—grandparents, brothers and sisters, aunts, uncles, and cousins. And within these extended families, one man was often designated as a *gaal*—a kinsman-redeemer.

The kinsman-redeemer ensured the family's security and stability. According to the Law, kinsman-redeemers were to buy back lands that were sold to settle a debt (Leviticus 25:25), had the first right of refusal to purchase land within the family (Ruth 4:1–6), were responsible to buy back family members who sold themselves into slavery to pay debts (Leviticus 25:47–49), were accountable to avenge the murder of a family member (Deuteronomy 19:12), and could marry the childless widow of a near kinsman—a brother or one related by marriage.

The story of Ruth and Boaz centers on this last responsibility of the kinsman-redeemer. Another man was a closer *gaal* than Boaz and had the legal right to either accept or reject his right to marry Ruth. On the night that Ruth came to Boaz, he wisely told her that he would speak to the close relative, and if that kinsman refused to marry her, then he would fulfill the role of *gaal*.

Related passages: Deuteronomy 19:1–13; Jeremiah 32:6–8; Matthew 22:24

4:1 Sitting at the Gate

In the ancient world, everyone who was anyone hung out at the city gate. As the initial entrance into a city, the gate was the center of civic, social, and legal affairs. Elders and judges, as well as law enforcers, sat at the gate as a sign of their wisdom and stability. In some cases, the king's throne was even moved to the gate when a kingdom wanted to emphasize its control over the

Ancient city gate in Gezer

city. Some kings also piled the heads of their vanquished enemies at the gate to show off their wartime prowess.

Places at the gate were the exclusive domain of men. And the men who congregated at the gate were in the highest social strata. Boaz was a well-respected citizen of Bethlehem. When he decided to marry Ruth, he went to the city gate to speak to Naomi's "closest relative" (Ruth 4:1, 3). Gathering at least ten elders of the city at the gate, Boaz called them to bear witness that the near kinsman would give up his claim to purchase the land of Elimelech, Naomi's deceased husband, and thereby free Boaz to marry Ruth (4:2–6).

Related passages: Genesis 34:20; Deuteronomy 22:15; Job 29:7

4:7–8   A Strange "Handshake"

Feet may not be the most attractive aspects of the human body. But like other bodily parts, feet need protection from the elements. In the ancient world, the most common type of footwear was the sandal. Sandals were

Replicas of ancient sandals

typically made of leather, with a strap or thong to securely fasten it to the foot. So lowly was the foot and so common was the sandal that it was considered a symbol of insignificance (Genesis 14:23) and to loosen someone's sandal thong was considered the task of the lowly (John 1:27).

Removing one's sandal also indicated a sign of reverence during worship (Exodus 3:5). And in the book of Ruth, we find the curious practice of removing one's sandal in a business transaction. The author stated this was a common custom in ancient Israel (Ruth 4:7). It might be analogous to a brother-in-law refusing to fulfill the obligation of levirate marriage, whereby the widow could then remove the sandal from her brother-in-law's foot and spit in his face. The episode in Ruth gives us no indication that either Boaz or the close relative spat. But after refusing to buy back the land of Elimelech and thereby obligate himself to marry Ruth, the close relative of Naomi removed his sandal and gave it to Boaz as a testimony of his refusal, sealing the deal (Ruth 4:8). Today, we might say he "signed on the dotted line," or he gave his word and "shook on it."

Related passage: Deuteronomy 25:8–10

FIRST SAMUEL

—❈—

1:3 Before Jerusalem, Shiloh

When we consider Israel, the city of Jerusalem immediately comes to mind. However, before Jerusalem served as the center of worship for Israel, God's people streamed to the tabernacle in Shiloh, a city in the hill country of Ephraim, nearly thirty miles north of Israel's current capital. Before Shiloh's destruction, the Israelites worshiped there for more than four centuries. Throughout history, God's people have associated worship with a physical place, a location that serves as a rallying point for the entire nation.

Joshua established the tabernacle at Shiloh just after the conquest (Joshua 18:1). The tabernacle remained in Shiloh for more than three hundred years. Later, David brought the heart of the tabernacle—the ark of the covenant—into Jerusalem (2 Samuel 6). During its tenure in Shiloh, the tabernacle drew people together for the Law's prescribed annual feasts, such as Passover and the Feast of Tabernacles (1 Samuel 1:3). Further, the Israelites added on to the tabernacle, including doorposts (1:9) and doors (3:15). The Philistines captured the ark and held it for a short time, after which it remained at Kiriath-jearim until David brought it up to Jerusalem (1 Samuel 4:3; 2 Samuel 6:12).

Related passages: Judges 18:31; Psalm 78:60

5:2   Da-gon!

Dagon, the god of the Philistines, shows up in the Bible during the period of the judges, before the monarchy was established. The Philistines believed Dagon ruled over the grain crops that they grew in

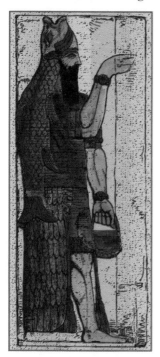

the wide valleys to the southwest of Israel. When the Philistines captured Samson—who had killed their people and burned their crops (Judges 15:5, 8)—they offered a sacrifice and gave thanks to Dagon for delivering them from the destroyer of their country (16:23).

Dagon's most significant entry into the biblical narrative comes in 1 Samuel 5, which recounts the capture of the ark of the covenant by the Philistines. The Philistines stored the ark in their temple devoted to Dagon. The next morning, the statue of Dagon had been knocked down and was bowing before the ark. The following morning, it had been dismembered and beheaded. When the Philistines began to fall ill, they sent the ark back to the Israelites.

Image of the god Dagon   *Related passage: 1 Chronicles 10:10*

8:11   The Chariot Waits for No One

Around 2500 BC, armies began to use chariots—two-wheeled vehicles drawn by beasts of burden such as oxen, horses, and donkeys. The earliest forms of the chariot consisted of a small platform with a wheel on each side and a pole used to attach the platform to the animal. As time passed, the axle holding the wheels moved to the rear of the chariot, while the front of the vehicle contained a light railing or solid piece designed to hold weapons such as arrows, spears, and battle axes. Most chariots of this type were drawn by two horses and included a crew of at least two men—one to drive and one to fight. Chariots were used not just in war but also in peacetime during processions as well as for travel (Genesis 41:43; Acts 8:28–29).

Perhaps the most famous appearance of chariots in Scripture involved in the Egyptian pursuit of Israel during the exodus (Exodus 14:6). The "iron chariots" of the Canaanites could not have been made completely of iron due to the excessive weight (Judges 1:19). Instead, the chariots would have been outfitted with a few iron pieces to strengthen them for war. Such strong fighting vehicles made it difficult for the Israelites to move out into the plains during their conquest, and even through the days of the Philistines (1 Samuel 13:5). Samuel promised the Israelites that they would be forced to populate the king's army with charioteers, a prediction which became reality under the reign of David (8:11; 2 Samuel 8:4). In Israelite history, chariots were more common in the northern kingdom, which had more open plains (1 Kings 16:9).

Related passages: Genesis 46:29; Psalm 20:7

8:13   Sweet-Smelling Traditions

Perfumers generated a great deal of business in the hot climate of the ancient Near East. People sought to deal with the fetid effects of high temperatures by applying perfumes to their bodies after bathing. The varieties of perfumes were almost endless, being derived from any number of plants. Some perfumes came in powder form and would have been kept in bags (Song of Solomon 1:13). Other perfumes came in liquids and ointments and would have been kept in boxes or jars (Isaiah 3:20; Matthew 26:7). In the Bible, we see people apply perfumes to the feet (Luke 7:38), the lips (Song of Solomon 5:13), and the body (Ruth 3:3). Any wealthy person would have had access to perfume, with the king even employing his own perfumers (1 Samuel 8:13). Perfumes were also used on the bodies of those who had recently died in order to mask the inevitable smell (John 19:39).

Related passages: Exodus 37:29; 2 Chronicles 16:14

11:15   Israel Camped at Gilgal

The name Gilgal—probably derived from a term for "circle"—can refer to at least two distinct cities or villages appearing in the Old Testament. The most prominent and frequently mentioned Gilgal lies near Jericho on the Jordan River. When Joshua led the Israelites across the Jordan, they camped first at Gilgal (Joshua 4:19), where they circumcised their people and celebrated the Passover (5:8, 10). Because of its historical importance, this location took on a sacred significance during Israel's time in the land. When Samuel traveled from city to city as leader of Israel, he included Gilgal on his three-city tour, indicating its importance as a meeting center for the people (1 Samuel 7:16). This Gilgal was also the location where Samuel pronounced Saul the first king of Israel (11:14–15). The Bible mentions other villages named Gilgal in Deuteronomy 11:30; Joshua 12:23; and 2 Kings 2:1–4.

Related passages: Joshua 9:6; Judges 3:19

14:20   Swords and Daggers

There were two different types of sharp, double-edged, offensive weapons in the ancient Near East. The smaller of these was a dagger, which Ehud the judge used in his attack of the wicked King Eglon (Judges 3:16, 21–22). The longer blade, also double-edged, was called a sword, first appearing in biblical combat when Simeon and Levi attacked the Shechemites in defense of their sister's honor (Genesis 34:25). Sword lengths varied in the ancient world. The swords of Israelite men like Gideon, Saul, and David (Judges 7:14; 1 Samuel 14:20; 25:13) would have been shorter than average, possibly as short as twenty inches in length. Swords in the biblical period were made from metals such as bronze, copper, gold, and iron. Often, decorative handles were attached, some made of ivory or studded with silver. People generally carried swords in sheaths or scabbards to protect the blades . . . and themselves.

Related passages: Proverbs 5:4; Jeremiah 47:6

17:40   Taking a Shot

Israelite armies used the slingshot regularly during the Old Testament era. Slings were usually woven or cut from wool, rope, or leather. Inexpensive and easily carried, the slings allowed Israelite soldiers to throw stones the size of a man's fist up to a hundred miles per hour, giving this simple weapon lethal potential. David stands as the most famous sling-thrower in the Bible, as he used the weapon in his fight against the Philistine giant Goliath (1 Samuel 17:48–50). The smooth shape of the stones David collected from a nearby brook allowed them to fly faster through the air. The Bible offers plenty of evidence that others in Israel made use of this weapon, including the seven hundred left-handed slingers of Benjamin (Judges 20:16) and slingers in the siege of Kir-hareseth (2 Kings 3:25). Archaeological evidence supports the biblical evidence, with abnormally large numbers of stones surrounding the ruins of besieged cities.

Lachish sling stones

Related passages: 1 Chronicles 12:2; 2 Chronicles 26:14

22:6   Made for Shade

In many parts of Israel, the hot temperatures and dry conditions wear on even the hardiest travelers. Tamarisk trees dot the landscape of the Holy Land, and in ancient times, would have provided ample shade for individuals, caravans, and flocks moving from place to place. In general, tamarisks are large, leafy trees that easily provide cover from the sun. In the mornings, tiny water droplets often hang from tamarisk branches, meaning an even cooler environment for those under the tree's shelter. Abraham planted a tamarisk tree in Beersheba, near a well he had claimed as his own (Genesis 21:33). A tamarisk tree in King Saul's home-town of Gibeah was part of the setting for an important event in his life (1 Samuel 22:6). As the king relaxed under the tamarisk's shade, he gave orders to kill the priests of Nob—the shade of tree offering a striking contrast between the comfort of Saul and the discomfort of God's faithful servants.

Related passage: 1 Samuel 31:13

23:29   En Gedi

Located in an otherwise unforgiving wilderness area bordered by moun-tains on one side and the undrinkable Dead Sea on the other, En Gedi marks the site of spring-fed streams. At En Gedi, fresh water, foliage, and shade are abundant, creating a natural oasis for weary desert travelers. En Gedi's status as an oasis made it significant and well-known in that part of the world. But its remote location, along with the extremely hot temperatures, meant that there was never an overwhelmingly large settle-ment in the area. The ancient historian Josephus leads us to believe that about one thousand people lived at En Gedi in the New Testament era.[1]

En Gedi shows up in the Bible several times, most notably as the place where David took refuge in his flight from the murderous King Saul (1 Samuel 23:29). We also read that several nations attempted to invade Judah by way of En Gedi, a potential weak point—due to its isolation—in an otherwise formidable Judean defense (2 Chronicles 20:1–2). The invasion prompted King Jehoshaphat to seek the Lord and offer one of the great prayers of the Old Testament, resulting in Judah's defending itself from invasion.

Waterfall at the oasis of En Gedi

Related passage: Ezekiel 47:10

28:7   Which Witch?

Often called the Witch of Endor, the woman Saul visited near the end of his life should more accurately be called a medium. Essentially, mediums relayed messages from the dead to the living. The practice of acting as a medium was clearly outlawed in the Mosaic Law (Leviticus 19:31; 20:27), suggesting that mediums were common enough for God to create a protection from them for His people. Those visiting a medium would have brought some sort of offering or sacrifice, and the result would have been a conversation mediated by the medium, rather than a direct conversation between the dead and the living. This was certainly the case during Saul's visit to the medium at Endor (1 Samuel 28:7–14), an act which epitomized the disobedience for which he died (1 Chronicles 10:13).

Related passages: Leviticus 20:6; 2 Kings 21:6

SECOND SAMUEL

—❈—

1:17–27 The Song of the Bow

King David's expression of mourning for his best friend, Jonathan, and Jonathan's father, King Saul, took the form of a poem (2 Samuel 1:19–27). Many believe that the lost book of Jashar recorded King David's poem and might have given it the title: "The Song of the Bow." This title may have referred to Jonathan's skillful use of the bow as a weapon, as well as to King Saul's death at the hands of archers.[1] For example, 2 Samuel 1:22 says,

> "From the blood of the slain, from the fat of the mighty,
>
> The bow of Jonathan did not turn back,
>
> And the sword of Saul did not return empty."

Related passage: Joshua 10:13

6:6–11 Uzzah and the Ark

Second Samuel 6:6–11 records King David's attempt to transport the ark of the covenant to Jerusalem. When King David's men reached the threshing floor of Nacon, Uzzah reached out his hand to steady the ark. God killed Uzzah on the spot. Why did God react so harshly?

God's wrath may seem severe, but He exercised much grace and patience as King David and his men mishandled God's dwelling place. God overlooked two sins as His ark traveled to Jerusalem: the wrong people carried the ark, and they didn't carry it correctly.

God had assigned the Kohathites the job of carrying His holy things, including the ark (Numbers 4:15). The Bible never identifies Uzzah and Ahio as Levites or as Kohathites. The fact that God allowed the men to trek as far as Nacon's threshing floor shows His mercy.

Not only did non-Kohathites carry the ark, but they didn't follow God's prescribed method of transportation. God had commanded the Kohathites to carry the ark using long poles that rested on their shoulders. But King David allowed Uzzah and Ahio to haul the ark of the covenant on a cart pulled by oxen.

Finally, Uzzah grabbed the unsteady ark, and God lashed out against him. God had warned the Kohathites that if they touched the ark, they would die (4:15). The ark of the covenant wasn't just a pretty box to hold the Ten Commandments—God's presence dwelled in it, and He was enthroned

Image of Uzzah reaching to steady the ark of the covenant

between the cherubim (2 Samuel 6:2). God's presence made the ark holy, and He demanded that His people not treat His holy dwelling place with irreverence by touching it.

Related passage: 1 Chronicles 13:1–14

6:14–21   Dancing David

What did it mean that King David danced before the Lord, and why did it make his wife, Michal, so angry? How did the Israelites and the wider ancient Near Eastern culture view dancing?

This particular Hebrew word for dancing occurs only in this passage of Scripture, but it also means "play" in the Ugaritic language.[2] In Ugaritic, this word may have had sexual connotations, but David expressed only morally pure joy before the ark. In 2 Samuel 6:14–16, the king worshiped the Lord by "leaping and dancing" with all his might.

First Chronicles 15:29 uses a different word for *dance* in its account of King David's celebration; he made merry, expressing gladness before God.

In Israel, dancing usually accompanied religious festivals. When victorious troops returned from holy war, women danced to praise God for giving them victory and to honor the brave soldiers (Exodus 15:20). In Israel, dancing did not occur at burials or during times of mourning. In fact, the psalmist contrasted dancing and mourning to describe opposite feelings and realities (Psalm 30:10–12). On the other hand, Egyptian and Babylonian funerals often combined dancing and mourning.

Dancing also accompanied pagan prophetic rituals. The Baal prophets limped around the altar ecstatically on Mount Carmel as they wailed and cut themselves attempting to force Baal to act (1 Kings 18:21–26). Interestingly, Baal Marqad, the Baal deity of Lebanon, means "lord of the dance."

King David's wife, Michal, loathed her husband when she saw him dancing. But her hatred most likely stemmed from his scant dress—a linen ephod—rather than from his dance moves (2 Samuel 6:20–21).[3]

Related passage: 1 Chronicles 15:25–16:3

8:2   He Made the Moabites Do What?

After defeating and capturing the Moabites, King David used an unusual method to determine which captives would live and which ones would die. Although 2 Samuel 8:2 says King David "made them lie down on the ground," this may have metaphorically meant that he lined them up. Other verses use this language in the context of measuring and dividing land.

Regardless whether King David made the Moabites stand up or lie down, he counted off two-thirds of the captives and killed them. The remaining one-third he turned into slaves. The Moabite slaves then paid King David tribute, implying that Moab became a vassal state to Israel. As a vassal, Moab claimed a subordinate role to Israel, and Moab's ruler paid homage and tribute (tax) to King David.

Related passage: 1 Chronicles 18:2

10:5   Clean-Shaven and Ashamed

Following the death of King Nahash of Ammon, King David sent his servants to console the king's son, Hanun. But Hanun assumed that David's actions were disingenuous, so Hanun shaved the servants' beards and sent them home. When King David heard about this humiliation, he instructed his servants to stay at Jericho until their beards grew back (2 Samuel 10:1–5).

But why did King David make his servants stay outside Jerusalem just because their beards had been shaved? Just as long hair adorning a woman signified femininity, a beard on a man signified masculinity. Among the Israelites, God intended men to grow beards and women to have long hair, except in certain circumstances. The Bible instructed men and women to shave if they had a skin disease and had to follow a purification ritual (Leviticus 13:28–31). Men and women also shaved their hair during periods of mourning (Deuteronomy 21:12). Vows, such as those kept by Nazirites, prevented men from shaving their heads or beards until their vow expired, except in cases of defilement (Numbers 6:5–9).[4]

Jewish man with a beard

While God instructed the Israelites not to shave except in certain circumstances, some other nations had different policies on facial hair. Egyptian men were clean shaven, although royal officials sometimes wore fake beards. Assyrian and Babylonian officials often had beards.[5]

God intended a man's beard to show his maturity and masculinity. So, in the case of King David's servants, when Hanun mutilated the beards of King David's servants and sent them back to Jerusalem, he intended to humiliate and insult David's men. Out of respect for these men, King David instructed them to wait at Jericho until their beards—and their dignity—had been restored.

Related passages: Leviticus 19:27; 21:5

11:1 Commander in Chief

Although the Lord of Hosts intended to act as Israel's religious, moral, and military leader, He handed over these rights to human kings. God, therefore, intended the king to lead the army in battle. As the commander in chief, King David should have fought alongside his people against the Ammonites, but instead he stayed home.

In the ancient Near East, pagan kings represented gods to the people, and their role was to placate the gods on the peoples' behalf. The false gods of the nations constantly warred against each other, vying for control and trying to usurp the other gods' power. It would have been unthinkable for a pagan king to remain at home while his army went to war.

In Israel, the king ruled the people according to God's Law and led the people in their submission to Him. The Old Testament uses several words for *leader*, often referring to the head of a tribe or to a military leader. But one particular Hebrew word, *nagid*, points to someone who was a political *and* military leader. In 1 Chronicles 13:1, this word refers to King David's military commanders. In numerous other verses, the *nagid* led the armies to carry out the king's strategy. But the Bible also calls Jeroboam (1 Kings 14:7), Baasha (16:2), and David (Isaiah 55:4) *nagid*, with the implication that these kings had ultimate political and military control. Though David served as the commander in chief of Israel, in 2 Samuel 11:1, he abandoned his God-given duty, stayed home, and got into trouble with Bathsheba.

Related passages: 2 Samuel 7:8; 1 Kings 1:35; Daniel 9:25–26

11:2–5 Bathsheba's Infamous Bath

When King David should have been leading his troops in battle, he spent an evening on his roof enjoying the view. Regrettably, Bathsheba, the wife of Uriah the Hittite, chose this fateful evening to take a bath. But why did Bathsheba bathe on her roof?

Most of the bathing in the Old Testament was done as a part of cleansing rituals. Leviticus 15–17 prescribes ceremonial bathing for Israelites who had been defiled because of leprosy, touching something unclean, a discharge, or to prepare for the Day of Atonement. On the Day of Atonement, the high priest entered the Holy of Holies to present the sin offering on behalf of the entire nation. Purity was of central importance on this day.

The modern village of Silwan sits across the valley from the city of David. The buildings, built on top of one another, reveal how David could have seen Bathsheba that fateful evening.

But some of the wealthier Hebrews bathed for hygienic purposes as well. Often, only the upper classes had places to bathe, servants to carry water, and, therefore, access to non-religious bathing.[6] In the case of Bathsheba, her bathtub was most likely in a private courtyard on the flat roof of her home, which would have been situated below David's hilltop palace.[7] Or she may have bathed outside because of the sweltering heat on that late-spring day.[8] Whatever the reason, David saw her, lusted after her, and sent for her. This great sin of adultery resulted in the deaths of Uriah and the first son of David and Bathsheba.

Related passage: Matthew 1:6

11:4 Feminine Purification in the Ancient Near East

The parenthetical statement, "when she had purified herself from her uncleanness," in 2 Samuel 11:4 shows the reader that Bathsheba completed her purification after her menstrual cycle before returning home. In other words, she was *not* pregnant when she visited King David. When she became pregnant, King David was the only possible father.

But what did Bathsheba have to do to purify herself? God's regulations prescribed in Leviticus 15:28–30 stated that a woman had to wait seven days following her monthly cycle or any other discharge and then present two doves or young pigeons to the priest at the entrance to the Tent of Meeting. During her period or discharge, a woman remained unclean and could not worship or sacrifice at the Tent of Meeting.

While this regulation may seem harsh, God demanded pure people and only sacrificial blood in the tabernacle. Leviticus 15:31 says: "Thus you shall keep the sons of Israel separated from their uncleanness, so that they will not die in their uncleanness by their defiling My tabernacle that is among them." The Lord wanted His people to separate themselves from the pagan nations that surrounded them—nations that didn't care about impurity or holiness. God set His people apart from the pagan peoples, who engaged in illicit behaviors and idolatry, so that the Israelites would testify to His holy character.

Related passage: Leviticus 15:13–15

11:9–11   Who Was Uriah the Hittite?

Uriah the Hittite faithfully served in King David's army and earned the honor of being one of his mighty men (2 Samuel 23:39). So how did a non-Israelite become one of the king's best warriors, fighting alongside God's people?

Uriah the Hittite joined God's people as a *proselyte*, meaning that, though he was a foreigner, he believed in God and chose to adopt His Law. He had to undergo circumcision and abide by Mosaic Law. In return, he became an heir of God's promises to Israel (Exodus 12:48–49). Uriah the Hittite married Bathsheba, the daughter of Eliam, who was also one of King David's mighty men (2 Samuel 23:8, 34). Uriah refused to have relations with Bathsheba while he was home from war out of loyalty to his fellow soldiers and a desire to maintain the ritual purity required by the Law.[9]

God prevented some people groups from joining Israel. The Moabites and Ammonites could not join Israel "to the tenth generation," a figurative way to say forever (Deuteronomy 23:3–6).

Related passage: 1 Kings 15:5

16:21–22   The Harem and the Throne

He who controls the harem, controls the throne. King David's son Absalom put this theory to the test. Absalom's insolent actions with his father's harem revealed a blatant rebellion. Not only did Absalom's activity seal his political revolt, but it permanently severed his relationship with David. Absalom performed immoral acts on the roof, in the sight of all of Israel, in order to strengthen the support of those who had proclaimed loyalty to him. This sign showed that he had taken over his father's throne.

But Absalom wasn't the first to rebel in this way. In Genesis 35:22, Reuben slept with Jacob's concubine in order to prematurely claim his rights and inheritance as the firstborn. But because of this arrogant act, Reuben lost his legal status as firstborn (Genesis 49:3–4).

In 1 Kings 2:14, Bathsheba asked on behalf of Adonijah, King Solomon's brother, that a member of Solomon's harem be given to Adonijah. But Solomon responded: "And why are you asking Abishag the Shunammite for Adonijah? Ask for him also the kingdom—for he is my older brother" (1 Kings 2:22). King Solomon recognized that by asking for the hand of Abishag, Adonijah wanted to rule as king and, therefore, was in open rebellion against him.

Related passage: Genesis 35:22

FIRST KINGS

1:3–4 Nursing the Young and the Old

Registered nurses were unheard of in the ancient world, but nurses long held respected positions in ancient societies. The primary roles of a nurse were to suckle infants and to help rear them to maturity. Two well-known examples illustrate these functions: Pharaoh's daughter employed Moses's mother as a wet nurse for the infant Moses (Exodus 2:7–9), and Naomi took a leading role in caring for her infant grandson (Ruth 4:16).

Because nurses were so intimate with the children in their care, the nurse and child often became as close as family. When Rebekah left her father to marry Isaac, her nurse, Deborah, accompanied her for the journey (Genesis 24:59). And when Deborah died many years later, Jacob buried her and called the site the "oak of weeping,"*Allon-bacuth* (35:8).

But nurses did more than care for children; they also cared for the aged and infirm. In the case of the elderly King David, his nurse, Abishag, not only helped him with his daily needs but also slept in his bed to keep him warm at night. The author of 1 Kings pointed out that David was not sexually intimate with his nurse (1 Kings 1:4), indicating that while nurses cared for the physical needs of their adult charges, they were not concubines.

Related passages: Numbers 11:12; 2 Samuel 4:4; 1 Thessalonians 2:7

1:33, 38, 44 The King's Mule

When we think about the riding habits of royalty, we often think about horses. Our minds conjure up images of princes romping across polo fields on their ponies, kings and queens in carriages pulled by eight regal steeds, or even the return of the King of Kings and the Lord of Lords on His white war horse (Revelation 19:11–16). But the one equine that never comes to mind when thinking about royalty is the mule.

Mule

A mule is a crossbreed of a donkey and a horse — combining the strength and size of the horse with the endurance and surefootedness of a donkey. The characteristic stubbornness of the mule is proverbial today, but it was observed by David long ago (Psalm 32:9).

Israelites were forbidden to breed hybrid animals like mules (Leviticus 19:19), but they weren't forbidden to use them. Imported mules were highly valued in Israel and became associated with nobility. So, when David commanded Zadok, Nathan, and Benaiah to place Solomon on the king's mule, David was declaring to the nation his choice of successor.

After the Babylonian exile, mules no longer held the high distinction of carrying royalty but took on a lower role as beasts of burden (Isaiah 66:20).

Related passages: 2 Samuel 13:29; 18:9; 1 Kings 10:25; Ezra 2:66; Nehemiah 7:68

3:1 The Marriage of Politics and Idolatry

Marriage has always been a sacred institution. From the very beginning, God's ideal of marriage was one man and one woman living in an unbroken covenant relationship for a lifetime. But because of sin, humans often compromised God's ideal for marriage. When God's chosen people became a nation after the exodus from Egypt, God strictly forbade them from intermarrying with people from the surrounding nations (Deuteronomy 7:3; Joshua 23:11–13). However, the Israelites ignored God's command, didn't keep their sinful impulses in check, and married foreigners anyway.

Solomon is the classic example of one who violated God's command about intermarriage. Others in Israel may have disobeyed God due to an attraction to their foreigner spouses, but Solomon's marriages to foreign women were politically motivated—a practice not uncommon in the wider ancient world.

During biblical times, marriages were viewed as covenant relationships, not just between husbands and wives but also between families. In Solomon's case, as king of Israel, this covenant relationship between his family and the family of each of his wives took on added significance— it bound two nations together in a treaty. The great danger in these marriage alliances was that they usually led God's people into the worship of false gods, just as they did Solomon (1 Kings 11:1–8).

Related passages: 1 Kings 7:8; 9:16, 24; 2 Chronicles 18:1; 21:5–6

6:1–38   A Temple for Our God

King David's great desire was to build a temple for God (2 Samuel 7:1–7; 1 Kings 5:3). It was a dream unfulfilled. His son Solomon would build God's temple. But that didn't mean David couldn't do something for God; before Solomon ascended the throne, David gathered the necessary materials for building the temple (1 Chronicles 22:1–19).

The site of the temple in Jerusalem was at the threshing floor of Araunah, which David had bought for fifty shekels of silver (2 Samuel 24:18–25). This site is also known as Mount Moriah, the place where Abraham offered to sacrifice Isaac to the Lord (Genesis 22:2, 4; 2 Chronicles 3:1).

The Temple Mount in Jerusalem, the site of Solomon's temple

Construction on the temple began in the fourth year of Solomon's reign, in 966 BC, and took seven years to complete. The building itself was rectangular in shape, the longer sides running north and south (60 cubits; 1 cubit equals approximately 18 inches) and the shorter sides running east and west (20 cubits). The temple's height was 30 cubits. Proceeding from the east into the temple, the building was divided into three compartments: the vestibule or porch, the nave or sanctuary, and the inner sanctuary or the "Holy of Holies," each separated by beautifully carved olive wood or cypress doors inlaid with gold.

The sanctuary and inner sanctuary—not the porch—were surrounded by a three-story buttress containing storage rooms for the implements of worship and perhaps "apartments" for the priests. The upper rooms were accessed by a winding staircase.

The temple walls were built of stone, with a row of timber inserted after each third row of stone. The interior of the temple was paneled with cedar (and perhaps cypress, according to 2 Chronicles 3:5) and decorated with beautiful carvings. Though 1 Kings 6:21 and 6:30 say Solomon "overlaid" the walls and floor with gold, it probably means that the carvings were inlaid with gold.

Within the nave or sanctuary was the altar of incense (which was also made of cedar and overlaid with gold), ten golden lampstands divided equally between the north and south walls, and the golden table laid with bread as an offering to God (2 Chronicles 4:19).

Within the inner sanctuary or Holy of Holies was the ark of the covenant.

Solomon's temple was surrounded by at least two courtyards: one for priests and one for the laity (2 Chronicles 4:9). Within the inner courtyard—the priests' courtyard—stood two bronze pillars (1 Kings 7:15–21), the bronze laver supported by twelve bronze oxen used for washing the priests (7:23–26), ten bronze basins and their wheeled stands used for washing sacrificial animals (7:27–39), the bronze altar used for sacrificing (8:22), and a bronze platform on which Solomon stood and dedicated the temple (2 Chronicles 6:13).

Solomon's temple stood until 586 BC, when Nebuchadnezzar and his Babylonian army laid siege to Jerusalem, looted and burned the temple, and took God's people captive. Seventy years later, about 50,000 exiles returned to the land under the leadership of Zerubbabel and rebuilt the temple (536–515 BC). Later, beginning in AD 20, Herod the Great expanded the temple complex to accommodate additional construction and rebuilt the temple itself—the temple Jesus knew.

Related passages: 1 Kings 7:48; 2 Kings 25:1–17; Ezekiel 10:1–22; 24:21–27; Daniel 1:1–2

9:19 Ancient Distribution Centers

Every king in the ancient world was sensitive to how his kingdom demonstrated power and prestige. And a kingdom's power was measured by the size of its army, the number of chariots and warhorses it possessed, the lands it controlled, the magnificence of its capital city, the wealth of its treasury, and the number of storage cities within its borders.

Storage cities, or treasure cities, as they were sometimes called, served as sites for royal warehouses—and every significant kingdom during biblical times built them. For example, Egypt had storage cities in Pithom and Raamses (Exodus 1:11).

Typically, storage cities contained silos of grain, cisterns of water, and armories of weapons, including chariots and horses. Storage cities dotted strategically throughout a kingdom provided easy and efficient distribution of needed material and food during times of war or famine.

According to 1 Kings 9:19, Solomon had storage cities in Israel, such as at Megiddo, in Lebanon, and "in all the land under his rule," including the regions of Edom, Moab, Ammon, and Bashan.

Related passages: 2 Chronicles 8:4–6; 17:12–13

10:2, 10 The Sweet Smell of Success

Sweet spices were significant at the beginning of Jesus's earthly life. The wise men from the east presented the infant Jesus with gifts of frankincense and myrrh (Matthew 2:11). Sweet spices were significant also at the end of Jesus's earthly life. His followers prepared spices and perfumes to anoint His body for burial (John 19:39–40).

From the earliest days, spices were used to anoint kings, burned during times of worship, mixed with linen to wrap dead bodies, and applied

Various spices

as cosmetics or perfume. While some spices grew in Israel, most were imported from Arabia, Egypt, Persia, Syria, and present-day India. These included aloe, anise, balm, laurel, cinnamon, myrrh, and frankincense. The importation of these and other spices made them costly, and, therefore, usually exclusive to the wealthy, the noble, and the priestly class, who used spices in the service of God.

We don't know the specific kind or quantity of spices the Queen of Sheba carried in her caravan when she traveled twelve hundred miles from southern Arabia to visit Solomon in Jerusalem. But we do know that she presented him with "a very great amount"—camel loads—of rich, aromatic spices (1 Kings 10:2, 10).

Related passages: Exodus 30:22–25, 34–38; 2 Kings 20:12–13; Esther 2:12; John 12:3

10:11–12   A Forest of Exotic Trees

The queen of Sheba came bearing gifts when she paid Solomon a royal visit—camel loads of gifts. Along with great amounts of gold and spices, the queen of Sheba shipped in a forest of exotic trees—a "very great number of almug trees" (1 Kings 10:11).

Almug (or algum) trees were probably red sandalwood trees, which grow up to twenty feet tall. Because almug wood can be polished to a beautiful high shine, Solomon used these trees in the construction of the temple and in his palace. He also used the wood to make various musical instruments, including lyres and harps. Sandalwood is still used today for this purpose.

Related passages: 2 Chronicles 2:8; 9:10–11

11:3   Second-Status Wives

Solomon was a man of tremendous appetites—appetites that often led him to violate God's Law and to compromise God's ideal plan for relationships between men and women . This included Solomon's many marriages to foreign women and his taking concubines.

Concubines were slave women who were subject to legal, sexual relations with their male masters. Sometimes these women made up a king's harem, which existed solely for the king's sexual gratification. Other times, concubines served as maids to their master's wives, as was the case of Hagar, Bilhah, and Zilpah (Genesis 16:1–4; 30:1–13).

While possessing concubines was not sanctioned by God and was not His ideal for male-female relationships, the Lord offered legal protection to concubines and their children (Exodus 21:7–11; Deuteronomy 21:10–17). Many concubines were treated as second-status wives and were therefore treated well by their masters. Jacob even went so far as to make the sons of Bilhah and Zilpah coheirs of God's promise (Genesis 49:1–27).

Solomon's ancestors engaged in the practice of owning concubines and fathering children through them, but none of his ancestors had Solomon's financial means to care for three hundred concubines plus the children born to these women.

Related passages: Judges 19:1–9; 2 Samuel 21:10–14; Esther 2:14

11:7   Worshiping Moab's God

Moab was a thorn in Israel's side for a long time. And the worship of that pagan nation's god, Chemosh, eventually became the undoing of one of Israel's greatest kings—Solomon.

In addition to establishing an alliance with Egypt by marrying Pharaoh's daughter, Solomon made an alliance with Moab. At least one of his seven hundred wives was from Moab, and in order to satisfy her desire to worship her own god, Solomon built an altar to Chemosh. It was this shrine—which stood nearly three hundred years until it was destroyed by Josiah (2 Kings 23:13)—and other shrines erected to foreign gods that turned Solomon's heart away from God (1 Kings 11:9).

Unlike some other pagan gods, little is known about Chemosh or the practices of his cultic worship. He may have been associated with warfare. And sometimes he is linked to the goddess Ishtar (Venus).

Related passages: Numbers 21:29; Judges 11:24; Jeremiah 48:7, 13

The City of David (right) sits across the valley from the "Hill of Offense" (left), the "hill east of Jerusalem" on which Solomon built a high place for the worship of the god Chemosh

20:31–32   Sackcloth Garments and Rope Headbands

Despite its name, sackcloth wasn't made out of sacks. The English word *sack* comes from Hebrew and Greek words that have a similar sound and spelling—*saq* and *sakkos*. Sackcloth was actually woven from coarse camel or goat hair and worn against the skin, either as a loincloth or as a robe.

The most frequent mentions of sackcloth in Scripture reference garments worn during mourning or great sorrow. If the sackcloth was made of goat's hair, it was typically black in color, making it an appropriate illustration of the grieving individual's state of mind.

Wearing sackcloth could represent mourning for death, protest against wrongs, sorrow over sin, or submission to an authority. This final one is indicated in 1 Kings 20:31–32 with a twist. King Ahab of Israel had defeated the Aramean army, under the command of Ben-hadad. When it became clear that Ben-hadad and the remnant of his army could not escape Ahab, a group of Ben-hadad's servants approached Ahab seeking mercy. The signs of their submission were sackcloth worn around their loins and ropes worn on their heads—ropes Ahab could have used to hang them if he refused to show mercy.

Related passages: Genesis 37:34; 2 Kings 19:1; Nehemiah 9:1; Esther 4:1; Job 16:15; Daniel 9:3

SECOND KINGS

—⚜—

3:26–27; 16:3–4 They Did *What* to Their Kids?

The Israelites' pagan neighbors practiced human sacrifice, an evil act strictly prohibited by the Bible (Leviticus 18:21). The Moabites worshiped Chemosh, the sun-god. King Mesha of Moab feared defeat at the hands of the Israel-Judah-Edom alliance. So, in order to persuade his god to help his army, the Moabite king sacrificed his son—the heir to the throne—to Chemosh. But because Chemosh was a false god, even this extreme act didn't work.

Children were sacrificed to the goddess Tanit and the god Baal Hammon at the sanctuary called Topheth in the Valley of Hinnom.[1] The Hebrews also sacrificed their children to the Ammonite god Molech there (2 Kings 23:10; Jeremiah 7:31). Israelite King Josiah destroyed this and other idolatrous locations (2 Kings 23:10). Unfortunately, the Israelites followed in their neighbors' sin at other times and in other places (17:17). King Ahaz of Judah burned his son in the fire to Molech (2 Chronicles 28:3). King Manasseh followed this evil tradition and sacrificed his son too (2 Kings 21:6). In order to punish Judah for this kind of idolatry, God allowed Babylon to take them captive.

Related passages: 2 Chronicles 28:1–4; Jeremiah 19:4–5

4:34–35   Healing Rituals in the Ancient Near East

Odd healing rituals fill the pages of the Old Testament. Elisha lay on a dead boy twice, mouth to mouth, eyes to eyes, hands to hands (2 Kings 4:34–35). Isaiah placed a fig cake on Hezekiah's boil to heal him (20:5–7). And these remedies worked! Prophets of God spoke and acted on His behalf and according to His instructions . . . and relied on the Lord to work through them.

In contrast, superstition motivated much of the curative practices of the Israelites' pagan neighbors. These nations faulted evil spirits for illness, so they used spells, incantations, and magic in attempt to drive away these demons—and sickness. When widespread disease affected a people group, they abandoned their land—and the evil spirits that lived there—in search of a new home.

Israel's pagan neighbors also used medical remedies in attempt to cure disease. In Egypt around 1552 BC, doctors prescribed strange (and harmful) treatments for ailments: lizards' blood; putrid meat; stinking fat; moisture from pigs' ears; goose grease; and excrement from humans, antelopes, dogs, cats, and flies. They even recommended worms' blood and donkey dung to extract splinters, which often resulted in lockjaw, a symptom of the deadly disease tetanus.[2]

While pagans blamed evil forces for disease and used sorcery and unsafe remedies to dispel them, faithful Israelites prayed to God or sought one of His prophets for healing. Often the Israelites' sickness, epidemics, and famine came as a result of their disobedience to God's Law. If they repented, turned away from idols and rebellion, and returned to the Lord, He would heal them (Deuteronomy 32:39). God's prophets prescribed treatments for sicknesses, but they had God's sanction. And the remedies didn't include harmful substances. Ultimately, healing came from God.

Related passages: Matthew 8:1–4; Mark 1:30–31; Luke 5:17–26; John 9:1–7

5:14–17 Naaman's Dirt

Naaman commanded the army of
Syria under King Ben-hadad II.
The Syrians worshiped
Rimmon, the storm-god of
Damascus. Pagans in the
ancient Near East, including
Naaman, believed that certain
gods ruled over certain nations
but that they had limited
realms.[3] Naaman applied this
theology to Israel's God; there-

Mules carrying a load

fore, because he had received healing when the prophet Elisha told him
to wash in the Jordan River, Naaman wanted to take two mule-loads of
dirt from Israel back to Syria with him.

He intended to build an altar to the Lord and to sacrifice to Him and
no longer to the false gods of Syria. Unfortunately, Naaman's role was to
help the king of Aram as he knelt to worship Rimmon. So, in an effort
to honor God, Naaman planned to kneel on the dirt he took back from
Israel. Naaman professed, "Behold now, I know that there is no God in all
the earth, but in Israel" (2 Kings 5:15).

Related passage: Luke 4:27

6:16–17 Heavenly Armies

The Bible calls God "the LORD of hosts," but what does this mean? Nearly
all of the passages that use this title for God use it in a context of military
conflict. In 1 Samuel 15:2, Samuel called God the Lord of Hosts when
giving King Saul the command to completely destroy the Amalekites,
who had terrorized the Israelites while they journeyed from Egypt. David
relied on the Lord of Hosts to help him defeat Goliath the giant. In
2 Kings 6:17–18, Elisha identified "horses and chariots of fire." This represented the battle array of the "hosts" of the Lord, the heavenly army of

angels who fight on the Lord's behalf. Because these were spiritual beings, the servant could only see them once God "opened [his] eyes."

Pagans in the ancient Near East often relied on what they called a "host of heaven" to assist them in war. But this was different. The heavenly host often referred to a mythical council that included multiple gods and sometimes celestial bodies. This heavenly council argued, debated, and eventually made decisions about war and other important issues. The council appointed one presiding god, but no one god had ultimate, permanent authority.[4]

Unlike these pagan nations who relied on fictional, fickle gods with limited powers, the Israelites depended on the Lord, the Creator of heaven and earth, whose heavenly armies worked to achieve His perfect will.

Related passage: 1 Samuel 17:45

11:4   Who Were the Carites?

Jehoiada the priest hired the Carites to protect the new king, Joash, from Joash's evil grandmother, Athaliah. The Carites came from Caria in Asia Minor (modern-day Turkey). Many Carites worked as seafarers, but a number served as mercenaries — private soldiers hired for their expertise and skill.[5]

The Carites also appear in the Bible by another name, the Cherethites. The Cherethites maintained strict loyalty to the king, especially to King David. They protected David and served as captains of the king's armies (2 Kings 11:10), they assisted David when he fled from Absalom (2 Samuel 15:18), they chased Sheba when he cursed David (20:7), and they protected king-elect, Solomon, when Adonijah rebelled (1 Kings 1:38). The Cherethites' leader was Jehoiada's son, Beniah, which might explain why Jehoiada hired them to protect the temple and King Joash.

Related passage: 2 Samuel 8:18

17:24–28   The Beginning of the Samaritans

Second Kings 17:24–28 records how King Sargon of Assyria repopulated the area of Samaria in Israel after he carried away the captured Israelites. Sargon sent pagan people from Babylon, Cuthah, Avva, Hamath, and Sephar-vaim to settle in Samaria. Samaritans were likely the mixed-race people who came from intermarriages between these pagan groups and the few Israelites who remained in Samaria after the exile.

Mount Gerizim

The Samaritans were also a syncretistic people who mixed the worship of Yahweh with the worship of false gods. So, the Lord sent lions to kill some of them. To try to appease the Lord, they asked the king of Assyria to send one of Israel's priests to teach them the customs of God. One of the exiled priests returned to Samaria and probably took a copy of the Torah with him.[6] But this priest most likely taught the inhabitants the idolatry of Jeroboam (2 Kings 17:27–31).

The Samaritans changed a few words in the Torah and preserved it as their own. They replaced Mount Ebal with Mount Gerizim as the mountain where Moses commanded the Israelites to place the stone tablets upon which were written the words of the Law (Deuteronomy 27:1–4).

As time passed, the Samaritans began to worship on Mount Gerizim, at a sanctuary that they claimed Joshua built. Historians disagree on the actual date of this temple at Mount Gerizim. The first-century Jewish historian, Josephus, dates this temple to Nehemiah's time. Sanballat, a civic official who opposed Nehemiah's work of rebuilding the walls of Jerusalem, most likely had Samaritan roots (Nehemiah 13:28).

Related passages: Ezra 4:2; Nehemiah 13:28–29

18:4   Nehushtan the Bronze Serpent

During the Israelites' time in the wilderness, after their exodus from Egypt, God punished His people for grumbling against Him by sending poisonous snakes among them. When the people repented, Moses asked God to relent—and He did. God instructed Moses to make a bronze serpent, mount it on a stick, and hold it up before the people. Anyone who looked to the serpent and believed in God's power to heal would live, even though a poisonous snake had bitten him or her (Numbers 21:4–9). The Israelites eventually turned this symbol of God's grace into an idol.

In 2 Kings 18:4, righteous King Hezekiah destroyed the pagan idols and altars that past kings had built, as well as Moses's bronze serpent, which the Israelites worshiped and named Nehushtan. In Hebrew, the name Nehushtan sounds like the words for "bronze," "snake," and "unclean thing." [7]

During the Israelites' time in Egypt, they likely learned about Egyptian amulets—articles made of precious stones or gold and worn as necklaces, as earrings, or on clothing. These objects were believed to be endowed with special protective powers and often pictured deities.[8] In a similar fashion, the Israelites, God's chosen people, looked to a created object when they worshiped Moses's bronze serpent as their savior. Instead of following pagan ways, they should have trusted in the one true God to protect them from sickness, disease, and death.

Related passage: John 3:14–15

22:14–20   Huldah the Prophetess

When King Josiah's priest and scribe found the missing book of the law, he mourned because of the Israelites' disobedience. Josiah told Hilkiah the priest, Shaphan the scribe, and several other men to ask the Lord what He wanted them to do in response to the book. So, these men went to Huldah the prophetess, believing that she would give them God's words on the matter.

Huldah the prophetess was the wife of Shallum, who was the keeper of the priests' wardrobe and probably the prophet Jeremiah's uncle.[9] She spoke on behalf of God and told King Josiah's men the Lord would punish Israel for committing idolatry and disobeying His Law. But her words assured the men that God wouldn't unleash His wrath until after the death of King Josiah, who desired to obey God and had a humble heart toward Him (2 Kings 22:18–20).

In the ancient Near East, people believed that prophets and prophetesses spoke words from the gods to address timely social and political issues. Prophetesses delivered messages from Ishtar and other false gods and goddesses, and sometimes received these messages through dreams. But unlike the Israelite prophets and prophetesses, their pagan counterparts used divination

The Huldah Gates at Jerusalem's Temple Mount

to obtain their divine oracles.[10] God prohibited divination, sorcery, and communication with the dead. He spoke directly through the prophets and prophetesses of Israel.

Related passage: 2 Chronicles 34:22–29

23:11   Chariots on Fire

Second Kings 23 tells of King Josiah's reforms. He destroyed the horses and chariots that the kings of Judah had dedicated to the sun. What was so significant about this?

Many pagan peoples worshiped the sun, moon, and other celestial hosts. The Egyptians bowed to Re, the sun-god. The Assyrians worshiped the sun and all the heavenly bodies. The Babylonians in Mesopotamia (an ancient land between the Tigris and Euphrates Rivers) worshiped Shamash, the male sun-god, while in Ugarit (a city near the modern Syrian coast) people revered Shapash, the female sun-goddess.[11]

Mosaic Law prohibited worship of any created thing. The Israelites could bow to the Lord alone. Regrettably, several evil kings of Judah had succumbed to the influence of Assyria's religion, which included sun-worship. These kings built altars, employed priests, and dedicated chariots to the sun. They put their hope in the fiery body that the one, true God had created. When King Josiah of Judah came into power, he cleansed God's temple, burned the chariots, and destroyed the vessels and high places the Israelites had made to worship the sun (2 Kings 23:4–11).

Related passage: Ezekiel 8:16

Various Verses   Taxation without Representation

When one nation conquered another, the defeated king often became a vassal to the conquering king. The vassal king played a subservient role to the victorious king, or suzerain. Vassals maintained some autonomy but had to pay tribute, or tax, to the suzerain. The yearly tribute tax kept the vassal dependent on and in subjugation to the suzerain; the tax also increased the wealth of the suzerain. Failure to pay tribute on time amounted to rebellion and often resulted in a military attack.[12]

The following biblical examples explain the several times when the kings of Israel served as either a vassal, paying tribute to a stronger king, or as a suzerain, receiving tribute from a weaker king.

In 2 Kings 3:4–5, Mesha king of Moab paid tribute to Israel but rebelled after the death of King Ahab. In 2 Kings 16:7–9, King Ahaz of Judah sought Assyria's help against the kings of Aram and Israel. Ahaz gave to King Tiglath-pileser of Assyria gold and silver from the Lord's temple, promised to serve him, and became his vassal. But when Ahaz's God-fearing son, Hezekiah, took over as king, he rebelled against Sennacherib, Tiglath-pileser's successor as king of Assyria (2 Kings 18:7).

In 2 Kings 17:3–4, King Hoshea of Israel served as a vassal and paid tribute to King Shalmaneser of Assyria. When Hoshea rebelled and stopped paying tribute, Shalmaneser imprisoned him.

Related passages: Judges 3:15–18; 2 Samuel 8:2–6

FIRST CHRONICLES

—❦—

6:57, 67 Seeking Asylum

Justice in the ancient world was often swift, deadly, and personal. While the Law prescribed certain crimes punishable by the community, justice for murder and manslaughter was to be administered by one called an "avenger of blood"—the nearest male relative of the deceased.

But to prevent blood vengeance from dissolving into a bloodbath between families, the Law prescribed that the Israelites establish sanctuary cities, known as cities of refuge. The book of Joshua designated six cities in which a manslayer might seek asylum: Kedesh, Shechem, Kiriath-arba (Hebron), Bezer, Ramoth-gilead, and Golan.

One who was involved in the direct killing of another, in order to escape the avenger of blood, might escape to one of these sanctuary cities. Once within the confines of the city, the accused could not be apprehended or punished without trial. To determine whether the homicide was intentional murder or unintentional manslaughter, the accused was escorted under protection to the community nearest the scene of the crime and judged by elders not related to the victim or the accused.

If the crime was deemed murder, the accused was immediately turned over to the avenger of blood and put to death. But if the crime was deemed manslaughter, the accused was immediately returned to one of the cities of refuge and required to live there until the death of the high priest. If the manslayer traveled beyond the limits of the sanctuary city before the death of the high priest and was caught by the avenger of blood, the avenger could administer justice without guilt of murder.

Related passages: Numbers 35:9–34; Joshua 20:1–9

9:1   An Empty Library

Regrettably, many books of history have been lost in the dustbin of time. In fact, looking at the names of missing books listed in the Old Testament is like looking at an empty library. Unknown to modern-day readers except in name, are these:

- The Book of the Wars of the LORD (Numbers 21:14)
- The book of Jashar (Joshua 10:13; 2 Samuel 1:18)
- The acts of Solomon (1 Kings 11:41)
- The chronicles of Samuel the seer, Nathan the prophet, and Gad the seer (1 Chronicles 29:29)
- The records of Nathan the prophet, the prophecy of Ahijah the Shilonite, and the visions of Iddo the seer (2 Chronicles 9:29; 12:15)
- The records of Shemaiah the prophet (12:15)
- The annals of Jehu the son of Hanani (20:34)
- The acts of Uzziah, written by Isaiah the prophet (26:22)

Also missing are official royal court records and registers, such as genealogies and census lists. These missing annals include the "Book of the Chronicles" (Nehemiah 12:23), the "Book of the Kings" (2 Chronicles 24:27), and the "Book of the Kings of Israel" (1 Chronicles 9:1; 2 Chronicles 20:34).

Some believe the missing annals mentioned in the Chronicles are a reference to 1 and 2 Kings, but that is not so. Both 1 and 2 Kings also refer to missing records. For whatever reason, the Lord decided not to preserve these books and annals, leaving us to wonder what might be found in these lost manuscripts.

Related passages: 1 Kings 14:29; 15:7, 23; 2 Kings 8:23; 12:19; 14:18; 2 Chronicles 16:11; 25:26; 27:7

Old scrolls

9:11   The Chief Officer of the Temple

When God chose Israel as His people and brought them out of the land of Egypt, He commissioned them as "a kingdom of priests and a holy nation" (Exodus 19:6). The whole nation was to represent its holy God before an unholy world. And within the nation itself, the descendants of one tribe were to represent God before His people. From the tribe of Levi, God commissioned His priests to the nation.

Broadly speaking, priests ministered before the altar of God, offered sacrifices, and taught the Law (Deuteronomy 33:8–10). Their divine calling was to establish, ensure, and maintain the holiness of God's people.

The servants of the temple were divided into three groups: high priests, priests, and Levites. All priests were Levites, but not all Levites were priests. The Levites who were not priests cared for the temple complex. Priests represented the people before God through the practice of offerings. And the high priest, called "the chief officer of the house of God" in 1 Chronicles 9:11, represented the nation before God when he entered into the Holy of Holies once a year to make atonement for the nation's sins.

Related passages: 2 Kings 23:4; Zechariah 3:1–5

9:17–32   Keepers of the Gate

Many in ancient Israel considered non-priestly Levites to be on the bottom rung of those who worked in and around the temple because they didn't offer sacrifices. But that didn't mean that the responsibilities of gatekeepers (also called "keepers of the thresholds of the tent" and "keepers of the entrance" in 1 Chronicles 9:19) were unimportant.

Being a keeper of the gate at the tabernacle or the temple had a long and distinguished history. As a child, the prophet Samuel served as a gatekeeper (1 Samuel 3:15). David appointed 212 gatekeepers under his reign, and by the time Solomon ascended the throne, the number exploded to four thousand (1 Chronicles 23:5). The primary responsibility of gatekeepers was to guard the tabernacle (and then the temple during and after Solomon's reign). Stationed on the north, south, east, and west sides of the tabernacle, gatekeepers ensured the security of the sanctuary. Their presence was a visual reminder to the people that entrance into God's presence came at a price: unlawful trespass was worthy of death (Numbers 3:10). Gatekeepers even slept around the entrance, locking the tabernacle in the evening and opening it in the morning. For this reason, gatekeepers were said to hold "an office of trust" (1 Chronicles 9:26). The man who guarded the east gate, the king's gate—usually the chief gatekeeper—carried the added responsibility of protecting the king's life whenever the king came to the tabernacle.

Other duties of gatekeepers included:

- Ensuring the security of the tabernacle treasury
- Ensuring the security of the utensils used in worship
- Ensuring the security of the furnishings used in worship
- Adding priests in the preparation of showbread used in worship

Related passages: 1 Chronicles 15:24; 26:1–28; 2 Chronicles 31:14–15; 34:8–13; Nehemiah 11:19; Psalm 84:10

10:3; 12:2   The Most Feared Men on the Battlefield

Warfare in the ancient world was intimate business. Swords, spears, and shields made combat a close affair—so close, in fact, a solider could smell the breath of his enemy. But some of the most deadly and feared men on the ancient battlefield fought at a distance. Who were these men? The archers or bowmen.

Unlike the brute hacking and thrusting of sword-fighting, archery was a special skill acquired over years of careful study and practice. Most archers learned their deadly trade as boys, graduating to larger and more powerful bows as they grew into manhood.

Bows were sometimes made from a single piece of wood, but for added strength and pulling power, craftsmen eventually began making bows with composites of layered wood and animal hides, glued together with resin. Arrows were made of smooth, rounded wood with feathered fletching and topped with either stone or metal arrowheads. Bowstrings were usually made from animal sinew.

Image of ancient archers

The accuracy and power of the archer's arrow easily pierced body armor, finding its deadly mark. And because kings were often surrounded by the most valiant warriors armed with swords or spears, the archer's arrow was the perfect means of delivering death to an enemy's king. A number of Israel's kings were either wounded or killed by the drawn bow of an archer, including Saul (1 Samuel 31:3; 1 Chronicles 10:3), Joram (2 Kings 9:24), and Josiah (2 Chronicles 35:23).

Related passages: Genesis 27:3; 48:22; Joshua 24:12; 1 Samuel 20:20, 35–36; Psalm 18:34

10:4–5 The Ethics of Falling on the Sword

Suicide, for millennia, has been considered an ultimate act of cowardice and a harsh reality for all those affected. After King Saul fell on his sword at Mount Gilboa, David mourned Saul's death and wrote in a lament: "How have the mighty fallen! . . . Saul and Jonathan . . . were swifter than eagles . . . stronger than lions" (2 Samuel 1:19, 23).

Certainly, the Bible doesn't skirt the painful issue of suicide but records a number of men who took their own lives or who requested that others kill them:

- Abimelech, who was struck in the head with a millstone dropped by a woman, told his armor bearer to run him through so that "it will not be said of me, 'A woman slew him'" (Judges 9:54).

- Ahithophel hung himself in his house (2 Samuel 17:23).

- Zimri, who thought he would be king, set fire to his house and was consumed by the flames (1 Kings 16:18).

- Jonah attempted suicide by requesting the sailors throw him overboard during a storm at sea (Jonah 1:12, 15).

- Judas, after betraying Jesus, hung himself from a tree (Matthew 27:3–5).

At least two instances of mass suicide in Jewish history are recorded outside of the pages of the Bible—both during the Maccabean revolt against Rome first at Gamala (AD 67) and then at Masada (AD 73).

Ethically, the Bible is clear that suicide—as with the taking of any life—is a violation of God's Law and His will (Exodus 20:13; Deuteronomy 5:17). Other passages used to support this position include: Deuteronomy 30:19; Job 1:21; Acts 16:27–34; 1 Corinthians 6:19; and Ephesians 5:29. Some argue that suicide isn't a violation

Mount Gilboa, Israel

of God's command, often citing the principle of laying one's life down for others and using passages such as John 13:37; 15:12–13; and 1 John 3:16. However, the Bible makes clear that there is an ethical difference between taking one's life and giving it up—between suicide and sacrifice.

Related passages: 1 Samuel 31:1–6; 2 Samuel 1:1–10

10:4–5; 11:39   A Bearer of Arms

Whether or not kings readied themselves for battle with the dramatic flair seen in modern film is unknown. However, every king or solider of means did have at least one personal servant who cared for his armor and weapons of war—the armor bearer.

Armor bearers were more than keepers of armor and arms. They also went into battle with their masters, carrying additional weapons. Armor bearers weren't necessarily expected to fight as soldiers but were called upon to dispose of wounded enemies either during or after a battle. And while their masters wielded elegant swords, threw javelins or spears, and strung their bows with arrows, armor bearers brandished thick swords and clubs.

Armor bearers are mentioned often in the Old Testament, accompanying Abimelech, Jonathan, Saul, and Joab.

Related passages: Judges 9:54; 1 Samuel 14:7–17; 16:21; 31:4–6; 2 Samuel 18:15; 23:37

11:23   Club Med

The weapon of choice for the Israelites was either the sword or spear, but a good strong club would do in a pinch. The Old Testament uses two Hebrew words in reference to clubs: *tothach*, a mace or a mallet, and *shebet*, a cudgel or war club.

War clubs, like the one used by Benaiah in striking down the Egyptian giant, were usually constructed of a stone or a ball of metal attached to a wooden handle. Clubs were crushing weapons, swung at the arms and legs to disable an opponent and at the head to kill an opponent. With the invention and refinement of helmets, blunt-force clubs lost their effectiveness in killing an enemy. Eventually, clubs became stylized symbols of authority, sometimes called a "rod of iron" (Psalm 2:9).

While clubs gradually became less effective as implements of war, wooden clubs continued to be used by shepherds to protect their flocks from prey (Psalm 23:4).

Related passages: Job 41:29; Proverbs 25:18; Matthew 26:47, 55

12:8, 24, 34   A Shield about Me

Warfare in the ancient world—and in the modern world—is not an affair of offense only. Defensive tactics must be employed. The primary means of defense for the ancient warrior was the shield. The type of shield selected depended on the battle situation, the type of offensive weapon used, and the origin of the soldier.

Shields had to be light enough to allow mobility for the warrior and strong enough to offer protection. Shields were constructed of leather, wood, and beaten metals like bronze. Two types of shields are highlighted in the Old Testament: a small shield used in hand-to-hand combat, covering about half of the body, and a large shield used during sieges.

Small shields protected a soldier against such offensive weapons as swords, battle axes, and spears. Shields of this type varied in shape depending on ethnic groups:

- Egyptians preferred a shield that was rounded on the top and flat on the bottom.
- Hittites used shields that were shaped like a figure 8.
- Syrians and Israelites employed rectangular-shaped shields.
- Greeks made the round shield famous.
- Assyrians also used round shields as their primary means of defense.

Siege shields, full-length rectangular shields, allowed Old Testament archers to fire arrows from cover as an army approached city walls. Because of the full-body protection these large shields provided, kings often used these shields when they rode into battle. Full-body shields were indicative of the Roman army.

Related passages: Psalm 3:3; Ephesians 6:16

Ancient shield

SECOND CHRONICLES

7:2 House of the Gods

In 2 Chronicles 7:2, the glory of the Lord filled His temple (His "house") after King Solomon's prayer of dedication. But what does that mean? Did God really dwell in a physical building?

In the ancient Near East, pagans built temples to house their gods. The sites of such temples often had strategic importance and reinforced the idea that the idols had specific locations in which they could exercise their power. And the temples not only confined the gods' influence; they housed the actual idols—objects made of wood and stone carved in the images of gods.

The one true God of the Israelites, unlike the false gods of their pagan neighbors, transcended His temple and the earth He created. He dwells in heaven and rules over all nations, all people, and all created things in heaven and on earth (Psalm 103:19–22).

After making a magnificent house for the Lord, King Solomon rightly exclaimed: "But will God indeed dwell on the earth? Behold, heaven and the highest heaven cannot contain You, how much less this house which I have built!" (1 Kings 8:27). The temple provided the Israelites access to communal worship and sacrifice. But God Himself didn't need a temple; He condescended to meet with His beloved people where they were.

Related passage: Acts 17:24

12:15   Prophets and Seers

Second Chronicles 12:15 mentions two historical books that chronicled the acts of Rehoboam, king of the southern kingdom, Judah. These two books recorded the accounts of Shemaiah the prophet and Iddo the seer. Who were these men?

Shemaiah the prophet spoke against Rehoboam's plot to attack the northern tribes who claimed loyalty to Jeroboam, king of the northern kingdom, Israel (2 Chronicles 11:2–4). Shemaiah's annals described the continual wars between the kings, even though God had forbidden Rehoboam from fighting Jeroboam (1 Kings 12:22–24).[1] God then spoke through Shemaiah to condemn Judah for disobedience and to pronounce His judgment: an attack from King Shishak of Egypt. Shishak made it to the border of Jerusalem, but when Rehoboam and his princes sought God's forgiveness, He relented, and Shemaiah related that Shishak wouldn't destroy Jerusalem (2 Chronicles 12:5–8).

Iddo the seer chronicled the reigns of Solomon, Rehoboam, and Abijah. Iddo condemned Jeroboam for burning incense on the altar in 1 Kings 13:1–10 and, according to Jewish historian Josephus, Iddo may have also been called Jadon or Jaddo.[2]

What distinguished Shemaiah as a prophet and Iddo as a seer? The difference between these offices was very slight. A prophet and a seer both spoke words from God, revealing past, present, or future events. The Hebrew word for "prophet," *nabi*, indicates a person chosen by God to receive messages from Him. The Hebrew word for "seer," *haza*, refers to a person who "saw" or "perceived" a revelation, dream, or oracle from God. The title "seer" was likely more popular during Israel's early history, while "prophet" may have been more popular in later years.[3]

Related passage: 1 Kings 12:12–13

14:9–11   The Million-Man Army

Second Chronicles 14 records King Asa's rule in Judah. Asa followed God, encouraged the people to obey His Law, and removed the high places—places set aside for the worship of false gods. During a time of peace, Asa fortified many cities in Judah and built an army of almost 600,000 valiant, well-armed warriors.

Then, according to 2 Chronicles 14:9–11, Zerah of Ethiopia led his army of one million men and three hundred chariots to the valley of Zephathah at Mareshah to fight King Asa. But when Asa prayed for God's help, God defeated Zerah's army.

Image of an ancient army

But did Zerah the Ethiopian really have an army of one million men, or does this number have symbolic meaning? Historians note that Zerah commanded the military of Osorkon I of Egypt, which did have a large army but most likely not one with one million men.[4] Often the designation "one million" indicated a vast number but didn't literally mean one million.[5] The NIV translates verse 11 of chapter 14 as, "a vast army."

Related passage: 2 Chronicles 16:7–8

20:14–17   The Empowering Spirit

In 2 Chronicles 20:14–17, Jahaziel—a Levite, a descendant of Asaph, and the son of Zechariah—prophesied to King Jehoshaphat of a looming attack from the armies of Edom, Ammon, and Moab. With the Spirit of the Lord upon him, Jahaziel instructed the king to march out to meet the enemy alliance but then to stand still because God would fight for His people. And He did. God ambushed the enemy alliance, throwing them into a confusion that ended with their killing each other (2 Chronicles 20:22–23)!

But what did it mean for the Spirit of the Lord to come upon Jahaziel? Unlike pagan priests and servants of idols who sought and sometimes achieved a state of possession by their gods, servants of the Lord *received* empowerment from the Holy Spirit. God gave power to His people in a controlled manner—a stark contrast to the chaotic possession that overtook pagan worshipers. Moreover, the gods of Israel's neighbors weren't gods at all (Deuteronomy 32:16–18). They were demons in disguise who desired to direct the actions of pagan worshipers in order to thwart God's purposes.

While the Israelites' neighbors sought frenzied possession by their gods, followers of God sought and continue to seek controlled, God-honoring empowerment by the Holy Spirit, the third person of the Trinity, who "came upon" Moses, Joshua, the judges, David, Solomon, Jahaziel, and others. Their testimonies reveal that when God calls people to His service, He equips them with the abilities, wisdom, and power to carry out His will.

Related passage: Psalm 106:36–38

21:18–20   Funeral Fire

Because of disobedience and idolatry, God struck King Jehoram with a horrible, unknown disease that turned his bowels into external organs: "Now it came about . . . that his bowels came out because of his sickness and he died in great pain" (2 Chronicles 21:19). And the judgment on Jehoram didn't end when he died in agony. His people also didn't honor him at his burial as they had other kings: "And his people made no fire for him like the fire for his fathers . . . and he departed with no one's regret, and they buried him in the city of David, but not in the tombs of the kings" (2 Chronicles 21:19–21).

Clearly, Jehoram received a dishonorable burial, but what constituted an *honorable* burial for the Israelites? Unlike the Egyptians who embalmed the dead, the Israelites anointed their dead with spices and ointments. They wrapped the deceased's hands, feet, and faces in linen cloths. Kings and wealthy Israelites were placed in family tombs carved out of rock. And although the Israelites did not normally practice cremation, fire played a part in their burials. Fires, like the one mentioned in 2 Chronicles 21:19, were set to honor the memory of the dead. Because the people recognized King Jehoram's wickedness, he received no honorary fire at his funeral.

These tombs in the City of David may be those of Judah's kings.

Related passage: 2 Chronicles 16:12–14

23:14 God's Holy House

After setting up young Joash as king of Judah, high priest Jehoiada ordered the Levites to protect God's temple and the new king, instructing them to kill the current evil ruler, Athaliah, but *not* inside God's holy temple (2 Chronicles 23:14).

For Israel's pagan neighbors, a temple constituted the residence of a people's god. Such residences often portrayed the gods' images, housed idols, and provided a place for cultic practices. Very few temples had separate "holy" rooms—rooms removed from the common people—for their idols. In fact, most had no developed sense of holiness whatsoever.

Unlike pagan temples, the Lord's temple had no idol, just the ark of the covenant with its mercy seat, which only one priest could access once per year. God's temple didn't limit His presence or His action. His temple was holy and separate from all pagan temples. And He expected the priests who ministered in His house to maintain holiness and ritual purity.

To keep them from defilement, common Israelites could not touch dead bodies, except those of close family members (Leviticus 21:1–3). But Leviticus 21:10–11 barred a priest from approaching *any* dead body, even that of his father or mother. Athaliah's dead body in the temple would have profaned God's priests and His holy house. Therefore, Jehoiada commanded the troops first to take Athaliah outside to the Horse Gate of the king's house and then to kill her.

Related passage: 2 Kings 11:15

25:14   Worthless Gods

Second Chronicles 25 records God's defeat of the Edomites on behalf of King Amaziah of Judah. After witnessing God's faithfulness and power, Amaziah grabbed some of the

The land of Edom

Edomites' idols, took them back home, and worshiped them. Ironically, Amaziah bowed before the same gods that couldn't save the Edomites. God's judgment on Amaziah resulted in his defeat at the hands of Israel's king Joash and, eventually, in Amaziah's murder.

Esau's descendants, the Edomites, lived in Seir (Edom). Although Seir's strategic location along trade routes between India, Arabia, Mesopotamia, and Egypt made it a beneficial site for commerce, the Edomites existed primarily as an agricultural people who worshiped several fertility deities. Because their livelihood depended largely on crop growth, they also sought out the gods they thought could control the weather.

Indeed, the Edomites revered many gods, particularly one they called Qaus, and they displayed idols in their homes.[6] Regrettably, after God gave victory to Amaziah's army, Amaziah took some of these household gods back to Judah and burned incense to them, which ultimately led to his downfall.

Related passage: 2 Kings 14:7

26:16–18   Incensed Over Incense

Pride has caused the downfall of many good people—including King Uzziah of Judah. After fortifying cities, building his army, and equipping them with the best armor and weapons, Uzziah defeated the Philistines, the Arabians, and the Meunites. But Uzziah, whose name means "the Lord is my strength," forgot that God gave him these victories. As a result, Uzziah took the credit, and pride filled his heart.

Nothing can stop a prideful man from doing whatever he wants to do. So King Uzziah entered God's temple and burned incense on the altar—an act reserved for the Levitical priests (Exodus 30:7–8). Knowing the command that a layman who performed priestly duties must be killed (Numbers 3:10), the eighty priests who knew of the king's stunt practiced restraint but courageously opposed him. When Uzziah stiffened his neck in anger against the priests, God struck him with leprosy—a skin disease that prevented Uzziah from entering the temple for the rest of his life (Leviticus 13:45–46) and brought him a less-than-honorable final farewell. As a leper, Uzziah was buried near, but not with, his royal ancestors (2 Chronicles 26:23).

Related passage: 2 Kings 15:1–7

32:30   Hezekiah's Tunnel

Until King Hezekiah's reign, Jerusalem didn't have convenient access to water inside the city walls; this put Jerusalem at a distinct disadvantage during a siege. Upon learning of an impending attack by King Sennacherib of Assyria, Hezekiah enlisted a team of engineers to build a tunnel connecting the Gihon spring to a pool inside the wall of Jerusalem (2 Kings 18:13–19:37). The Siloam Tunnel, constructed in the eighth

century BC, stretched more than 1,700 feet, and its shaft plunged as deep as 150 feet below ground. The sloped shaft directed the spring water into a pool inside the city wall (2 Chronicles 32:30). In order to build the tunnel, two teams of workers started at opposite ends, dug toward each other, and met in the middle. This amazing engineering feat still astounds experts today!

King Ahab built a similar water tunnel at Megiddo in the ninth century BC. That 200-foot underground structure had a shaft and winding staircase that descended 115 feet below the surface. The technology used by Hezekiah and Ahab most likely came from the Mycenaeans, via the Canaanites, around the fourteenth century BC.[7]

Water from the Gihon Spring still flows through Hezekiah's Tunnel today.

Related passage: 2 Kings 20:20

36:5–23   Fear Tactics

At the height of their power, the Assyrians alone had a standing army, and they maintained their power by employing fear tactics such as brutal massacres and deportation. Such threats kept enemies from resisting the Assyrians' imperialism and made vassal states think twice about rebelling.[8] The Babylonians, the superpower that replaced Assyria, added to their arsenal of fear tactics the capture of citizens from conquered nations—especially the most intelligent and talented citizens (Daniel 1:3–4).

Unfortunately, the Israelites had several altercations with the cruel Assyrians and Babylonians—and lost. Second Kings 17:7–23 recounts the Israelites' sin: idolatry, immorality, divination, and sorcery. God punished them by sending the feared Assyrian army, which destroyed Israel's cities and took most of God's people captive.

In 2 Chronicles 36:5–23, King Nebuchadnezzar of Babylon invaded Judah and took Judah's captives back to Babylon in three stages—605 BC, 597 BC, and 586 BC. Nebuchadnezzar also captured Judah's kings, first Jehoiakim and then his successor, Jehoiachin. The Babylonian invasions and deportations came as a result of God's judgment toward Judah for their neglecting the sabbatical year. God had commanded His people to let the land rest every seventh year, but for 490 years, they disobeyed (Leviticus 25:1–7). So judgment came, and while the Jews remained in captivity in Babylon for approximately seventy years, the land enjoyed rest (Jeremiah 29:10).

Related passages: 2 Kings 15:29; 24:14–16; 25:11–12

EZRA

1:1 Cyrus, My Servant

Cyrus II established the Persian Empire, expanding the territory under his control both east and west from Persia over the course of many years. After conquering the northwest as far as the Greek city-states of Ionia (now Turkey) and pushing east into the confines of India, the Persian Empire culminated in 539 BC with the conquest of Babylon in the west, which to that point had been the dominant ruling power in the region. In just over a decade, Cyrus II expanded the Persian Empire far beyond the scope of any previous empire in that part of the world and set up an organized government structure that kept the empire stable for two centuries.

Cyrus II stands unique among ancient foreign rulers, as his policy of tolerance toward the conquered yielded benefits for many people groups, none more so than the Jews. This Persian emperor allowed the people under his rule to continue their religious and cultural practices and even to return to their native lands, if they were displaced people. Therefore, a mere fifty years after Babylon had finally conquered and emptied Jerusalem of its inhabitants in 586 BC, Cyrus II issued a decree that the Jews were to return to Jerusalem from their exile in Babylon. Once the Jews arrived in their homeland, Cyrus II decreed that they would rebuild their temple that had been destroyed in the Babylonian conquest. Cyrus II even returned the valuable articles of worship that had been stolen by Babylon (Ezra 1:1–11). God had long planned for this important work of Cyrus II. Before he even came on the scene, Isaiah prophesied the king's pivotal role in the history of God's people (Isaiah 44:28–45:7).

Related passages: 2 Chronicles 36:22–23; Daniel 6:28

3:7   The Stronghold of Tyre

The Tyrians came from the city of Tyre, just north of Israel and located on an island just off the Mediterranean coast. The city's island location proved advantageous throughout its history, for while the Tyrians had no access to wood and fresh water on the island itself, history showed their occupation of the island to be nearly impregnable. Tyre's most famous king was Hiram I, who ruled during the ninth century BC at about the same time as Israel's King David. During this period, the Tyrians became known for their architectural prowess, building great temples in their own city, as well as contributing to both the palace and the temple Israel built in Jerusalem (2 Samuel 5:11; 1 Kings 5:1–18). The Tyrian participation in building temples continued after Israel's exile, as the people to the north again contributed to Israel's large-scale construction project (Ezra 3:7). Because of its defensible location, Tyre remained free until Babylon forced a payment of tribute in the sixth century BC and subsequently Alexander the Great destroyed the city in the fourth century BC (Zechariah 9:1–4).

Tyre

Related passages:
1 Chronicles 22:4;
Isaiah 23:1–17

3:7   The Cedars of Lebanon

As the land directly to the north of Israel, Lebanon sits on the coast of the Mediterranean Sea, with a mountain range serving as the north-south spine of the country. The Lebanon Mountains boast extensive forests, from which the famous cedars of Lebanon come. Solomon asked Hiram, king of the nearby city of Tyre, to bring cedar trees for the construction of the Lord's temple in Jerusalem (1 Kings 5:6). These trees were such an integral part of Solomon's temple that the Bible even refers to the temple as "the house of the forest of Lebanon" on multiple occasions (1 Kings 7:2; 2 Chronicles 9:16). This contribution to Israel's worship space explains why Lebanon shows up often in Scripture, especially as a synonym for fresh, vibrant, and thriving growth (Psalm 92:12; Song of Solomon 4:15). The biblical prophets often turned this imagery on its head, using the strong trees of the land as a warning of the power of God's coming judgment—not even the cedars of Lebanon will stand under His judgment (Ezekiel 31:15; Zechariah 11:1–3).

Related passages: Isaiah 33:9; Hosea 14:6

4:2   Esarhaddon of Assyria

Esarhaddon, the king of Assyria, came to power in a most memorable fashion. He was not the first son of his father, Sennacherib, and yet, Esarhaddon was named as his father's successor quite early in life. As this went against the cultural practice of the day—the normal pattern would have seen Sennacherib's eldest son succeed his father—Esarhaddon's brothers became jealous, leading to anger with their father. After the Assyrian army was decimated in its attempt to invade Judah, two of Sennacherib's children assassinated their father the king in an attempt to take power for themselves. Though many in Assyria supported the assassins, Esarhaddon immediately went on the offensive and stamped out all dissent, killing his brothers and some of their supporters. As king, Esarhaddon continued his father's policy of importing settlers into conquered regions such as Israel. In Israel, these settlers worshiped the Lord as well as other gods, further diluting the religious purity and, as the Assyrian kings hoped, the political power of the conquered people (2 Kings 17:24–33; Ezra 4:2).

Related passage: Isaiah 37:38

4:5   Darius of Persia

The Bible mentions three separate rulers by the name of Darius. Darius I, who ruled Persia from 521–486 BC, appears most often in Scripture. As a cousin to the previous ruler, Cyrus II, Darius I did not inherit his kingdom in traditional fashion. Instead, Darius I took the throne by overthrowing a usurper—a man posing as the previous king's brother. Darius

This cylinder seal shows an image of Darius I standing in a chariot and shooting arrows at a lion.

spent much of his reign quelling rebellion, and he is most noted historically for the devastating loss his army suffered in Greece at Marathon (490 BC). Darius I displayed tolerance to the Jews, just as his predecessor had, appearing in the biblical account as the ruler who ensured that Cyrus II's decree regarding the Jews was carried out (Ezra 5:6). When the local governor in Israel became concerned about the rebuilding of the temple, Darius found his cousin's decree addressing the rebuilding, which allowed the people to continue their work (Ezra 6:1).

Darius I should not be confused with Darius the Mede (Daniel 5:31; 6:1; 9:1; 11:1), who was likely a local ruler of Babylon, appointed by Cyrus II (Daniel 9:1). Neither do historians identify Darius I with Darius the Persian (Nehemiah 12:22), who was probably Darius II and ruled Persia several decades after Darius I.

Related passages: Haggai 1:1; Zechariah 1:1

4:7   Son of Xerxes

The son of Xerxes I, Artaxerxes (also called Ahasuerus in Esther 1:1), ruled the Persian Empire from 464–424 BC, including the days when Ezra traveled from Babylon to Jerusalem, after the temple had been rebuilt but when the people were still in need of religious reform (Ezra 7:6–7). Though the previous Persian ruler had supported Israel's reconstruction efforts, when Ezra returned, the people had stopped the rebuilding of the city under the order of Artaxerxes, recorded in Ezra 4:21. Only many years later did Artaxerxes allow Nehemiah and his group to return to Jerusalem and rebuild the walls to protect the city from evildoers (Nehemiah 2:1–8). In the biblical account, Artaxerxes comes across as a cautious ruler who sought control of all his territories and yet, over time, remained flexible to the wishes of his subjects.

Related passages: Ezra 7:11–26; Nehemiah 13:6

4:10   The Land of Samaria

The region of Samaria received its name after Omri, the evil Israelite king, selected the hill of Samaria as the capital of his kingdom (1 Kings 16:24). Before the days of Omri, biblical writers referred to the land around Samaria as "the hill country of Ephraim" because of its association with the Israelite tribe that settled in that area (Joshua 17:15). The region became so dominant that the biblical writers referred to the entire northern kingdom as Samaria (Micah 1:1). The region itself was located immediately to the north of Judah and to the south of Galilee, between the Plain of Sharon on the Mediterranean coast and the Jordan River on the east. Today, wide valleys still stretch across the northern portion of the region, while further south, the land becomes increasingly hilly.

The land itself, known throughout the Bible by different names, figures into a number of Old Testament accounts, including those involving Abraham (Genesis 12:7), Jacob (28:10), Joshua (Joshua 24:25), Gideon (Judges 6:33–35), and Jeroboam (1 Kings 12:20–26). The people who were settled in Samaria during and after the exile opposed the efforts of the Jews to rebuild Jerusalem (Ezra 4:10–16). However, under John Hyrcanus, Jews during the period between the Old and New Testaments took control of the land, destroying the city of Samaria in the process. This conflict set the stage for the oppositional relationship between Jews and Samaritans referenced in the New Testament when Jesus journeyed through the area (John 4:9).

Related passages: 1 Kings 13:32; Amos 8:14

4:13   Paying Up

In Ezra's day, travelers and traders paid customs and tolls for the privilege of transporting goods and using roads. Under this system, as well as an organized system of satrapies, the Persian Empire collected large sums of money from its territories. When local opponents decried the rebuilding of Jerusalem, they appealed to the Persian king Artaxerxes's reliance on these taxes, raising the fear that the Jews would not pay taxes if they felt they could defend themselves within their city (Ezra 4:13). Initially, the opponents' strategy worked (4:21), but Artaxerxes later reconsidered, giving special tax-exempt status to those involved in religious service (7:24).

Related passages: Ezra 4:20; Matthew 17:25

6:2   A Median Kingdom

Located in what today would be the northern part of Iran, the land of the Medes—called Media—was largely settled around 1000 BC. Subject to Assyria and Scythia for much of their first few hundred years in the land, the Medes only gained some measure

The Cyrus Cylinder records the monarch's policy of tolerance that allowed the Jews to return to Jerusalem and rebuild their temple.

of independence when they allied with Babylon around 615 BC. This alliance allowed the Medes to extend their kingdom to the north and the west. Their relative independence under Babylon lasted until the rise of Persia under Cyrus II, whose mother was a Mede. Though Persia conquered the Medes, Cyrus II's policy of tolerance — perhaps inspired by his heritage — allowed the Medes to remain in their land. Moreover, Cyrus II even placed many Medes in leadership positions throughout his empire. As a result, many refer to the Persian Empire as the Medo-Persian Empire.

Related passages: Esther 1:3; Jeremiah 25:25

7:6   Scribes

To understand scribes in the ancient world, one must first understand the vital importance of reading and writing in those cultures. As developed and relatively rare skills, reading and writing afforded scribes a crucial and needed role in society. At first, scribes merely copied existing documents or recorded the spoken words of important government officials and prophets (Jeremiah 36:26). In their early incarnations, scribes functioned as secretaries, handling various administrative responsibilities such as gathering troops (2 Kings 25:19) or keeping financial records (2 Chronicles 24:11). Later, because of scribes' ability to read and interpret the Torah (the Jewish Law), these men became close advisors to kings (2 Kings 18:18) and were closely associated with wisdom. Ezra, the best-known scribe in the Bible, filled his role as one "skilled in the law of Moses" (Ezra 7:6).

In the Old Testament, scribes were responsible both for making known the Law to the people (Nehemiah 8:1–8) and for teaching the Law to those who led the worship of the people — the priests and Levites (8:13). This emphasis on the Law carried over into the New Testament era, as the scribes mentioned in the gospels were those skilled in the knowledge and interpretation of the Torah (Matthew 2:4).

Related passages: 2 Kings 12:10; Luke 11:53

NEHEMIAH

───※───

1:1 Susa: The Jewel of Persia

Three capital cites dominated the Old Testament's skyline: Jerusalem in Judah, Babylon in Babylon, and Susa in Persia. (Though Egypt was important in the ancient world, the Old Testament mentions no significant capital city there.)

Among these capitals, Babylon stood as the most powerful and prestigious. But not even Babylon could survive leadership by a foolish king and opposition from a determined enemy. On October 12, 539 BC, the Medes and the Persians together diverted the Euphrates River, which ran through the heart of Babylon; passed under the city's wall; and entered through an unguarded gate. Once inside, they put the Babylonians to the sword, and Darius the Mede took the city (Daniel 5:30–31).

Darius—for whom historical information outside the Bible is sketchy—probably ruled from Babylon for a few years, but in 521 BC, he moved to the capital city of Susa on the plain of Khuzestan (located in modern-day Iran). A sprawling and bustling city on a major trade route, Susa became a center for commerce. During the reigns of Darius and his son, Xerxes, the city boasted palaces built of Lebanon cedar; a treasury

filled with gold, silver, and lapis lazuli; ebony and ivory objects from Egypt and Ethiopia; and marble sculptures from Greece.

When Alexander the Great and his army marched out of Greece in 334 BC to conquer the world, Susa was one of his first stops. And within three years, the Persian king Darius III succumbed to Alexander, making Susa—the gateway to Asia—Alexander's.

Rare cuneiform tablets refer to the conquests of Darius the Great (top), to the murder of Xerxes (left), to Darius III's defeat (bottom), and to a Persian queen (right).

Related passages: Esther 1:2, 5; 4:8; 9:6–18; Daniel 8:2

1:1; 2:1   Ancient Appointments

Since the creation of the sun, moon, and stars, humanity has learned to keep time. In agricultural societies, reading the heavens and understanding the seasons proved a vital skill. Possessing it often made the difference between a plentiful harvest and a scarce one—a difference which often determined life or death.

Once God prescribed certain festivals of worship during certain times of year, keeping time according to a calendar became even more important for the Israelites. Seeking to obey the Lord and offer sacrifices during the appropriate seasons, the Israelites developed a lunar, or thirty-day, calendar consisting of twelve months. Unlike our modern-day, Gregorian, solar-based calendar, which calls for adjustments and begins in the winter, the Hebrew lunar calendar begins in the spring.

The Old Testament uses three different nomenclatures to refer to Hebrew months: numeric, pre-exilic (before the fall of Judah to the Babylonians in 586 BC), and exilic/post-exilic (the seventy years of Babylonian exile and afterward).

Compared to Western, modern-day month names, these designations look like this:

Numeric	Pre-exilic	Exilic/Post-exilic	Modern-day
First	Abib	Nisan	March/April
Second	Ziv	Iyyar	April/May
Third		Sivan	May/June
Fourth		Tammuz	June/July
Fifth		Ab	July/August
Sixth		Elul	August/September
Seventh	Ethanim	Tishri	September/October
Eighth	Bul	Marheshvan	October/November
Ninth		Kislev	November/December
Tenth		Tebeth	December/January
Eleventh		Shebat	January/February
Twelfth		Adar	February/March

Related passages: Exodus 13:4; 1 Kings 6:1, 37–38; 8:2; Nehemiah 6:15; Esther 2:16; 8:9

1:2 A Remnant of a Remnant

For 490 years, the Lord's patience held out in the face of disobedience. God had commanded that every seventh year the land should have a sabbath rest and lay fallow (Leviticus 26:34, 43). But the people of Judah refused to obey and continued to work the land nonstop for 490 years. Their persistent disobedience regarding the Sabbatical Year, coupled with their persistent idolatry, brewed the perfect storm to bring divine judgment to Judah (Jeremiah 7:30–31).

In 605 BC, the Babylonian king Nebuchadnezzar marched through Judah, taking many captives. After another invasion in 597 BC, he came back in 586 BC, destroying Jerusalem and exiling additional captives. However, Nebuchadnezzar didn't take *every* man, woman, and child from Judah. Consistent with the practice of the ancient world, Nebuchadnezzar deported skilled workmen, artisans, the educated, and those of noble birth. But he left behind a remnant—those who "escaped" deportation. These "escapees" were the poorest of the poor who had little to offer Babylon.

Outside of what the book of Lamentations records, historians know little about the life of these escaped captives. But for seventy years, they scratched out a living in and around the destroyed capital of Jerusalem, until eventually, the deported captives began to return—first under Zerubbabel, then Ezra, and finally, Nehemiah.

Related passage: 2 Chronicles 36:20

1:11 Keeper of the Cup

Cupbearer may sound like the least glamorous of all the royal positions one could hold in the ancient world, especially compared to advisor to the king or captain of the bodyguard or even chief baker. But while *cupbearer* may call up images of a glorified waiter, the job was anything but boring and unimportant. In fact, the cupbearer was one of the most trusted and courageous men in the kingdom.

Ancient royal cup

The cupbearer's job description was simple but risky: taste the king's wine and food before it passed his lips to ensure it wasn't poisoned. For the cupbearer, this took courage, because the king's meal could be poisoned at any point during the preparation. For the king, it took trust, because the cupbearer could slip poison into the meal between his testing and the king's tasting.

Another job stress for the cupbearer: keeping up appearances. No king wanted to enjoy a meal in the presence of an ugly, glum servant, so cupbearers were chosen for their physical attractiveness and their positive personalities. Therefore, they could never enter the presence of the king looking disheveled.

The position also had its advantages. As trusted and intimate servants, cupbearers often gained political influence by serving as the king's counselors. This was certainly the case with Nehemiah.

Related passages: Genesis 40:1–5, 20–23; 1 Kings 10:4–6; Nehemiah 2:1–2

2:7, 9   The Ruler's Ruler

The Bible isn't just a religious book; it's also a political book. It deals with two of history's most important institutions: the temple and the palace, respectively addressing the spiritual and societal needs of humanity. Most people who read the Bible see the spiritual but miss the societal. However, much of Scripture revolves around kings, queens, and pharaohs. Daniel even took pains to list the governmental offices in Nebuchadnezzar's kingdom: satraps, prefects, governors, counselors, treasurers, judges, magistrates, and rulers of provinces (Daniel 3:2).

Mentioned throughout the Old Testament, the office of governor had a broad meaning. Generally, a governor wielded great political responsibility, serving as the head of a city, a province (a land with distinct borders), or a territory (a land with indistinct borders). Governors had broad powers, as did Joseph in Egypt. Often, they advised the king, as did Daniel in Babylon. And they all served at the pleasure of the king, executing and administering royal decrees.

During the Persian period, three governors ruled the province of Judah: Sheshbazzar under Cyrus (Ezra 5:14), Zerubbabel under Darius I (Haggai 1:1, 14), and Nehemiah under Artaxerxes I (Nehemiah 5:14).

As governor, Nehemiah traveled to Judah, passing through the provinces "beyond the [Euphrates]" (Nehemiah 2:7). To ensure safe passage, Artaxerxes I had to write letters to the governors of those provinces on Nehemiah's behalf.

Related passages: Genesis 42:6; 1 Kings 20:14–19; 2 Chronicles 34:8; Daniel 2:48–49

2:10, 19   Jerusalem Carpetbaggers

When Nebuchadnezzar carted away the leading citizens of Judah, he left behind a vacuum of leaders, artisans, and experienced workmen. But the poorest Jews remained, and struggling to make a living as best as they could, they were ripe for the picking by foreign and domestic carpetbaggers who set up shop in and around destroyed Jerusalem.

The book of Nehemiah names three of these parasites: Sanballat the Horonite, Tobiah the Ammonite, and Geshem the Arab. Sanballat was a local, probably from Beth-Horon about fifteen miles northeast of Jerusalem. He may have even been appointed as the governor of Samaria. Tobiah and Geshem were foreigners. As Nehemiah recorded in his book, Tobiah was from the eastern region of Ammon, serving as an official (perhaps the governor) of that province (Nehemiah 2:10). And Geshem was from the desert region of Arabia.

Sanballat, Tobiah, and Geshem opposed Nehemiah's rebuilding project, probably out of economic reasons. If Jerusalem had remained in ruins and the people had remained destitute, those three men would have controlled all trade between the Nile and the Euphrates Rivers.

Related passages: Nehemiah 4:7; 6:1–2, 6

2:13–15 Naming the Gates

Ancient cities were protected by walls, requiring gates scattered along the length of the walls to allow passage in and out. These gates' names reflected their geographic or functional characteristics.

Seventy years after Babylon's destruction, Jerusalem's walls and gates were in much disrepair. Nehemiah took on as his mission the rebuilding of the city. On his nocturnal reconnaissance of the city walls, Nehemiah referenced twelve gates by name:

1. The Valley Gate on the western wall leading to the Central Valley

2. The Dung Gate on the southern wall leading to the Hinnom Valley, the city's garbage dump

3. The Fountain Gate on the eastern wall close to the king's pool and garden, near the Pool of Siloam

4. The Water Gate on the eastern wall just above the Gihon Spring

5. The Gate of the Guard on the eastern wall close to the court of the guard near the king's house, just east of the Temple Mount

6. The Horse Gate on the eastern wall, just south of the temple complex (The significance of its name is lost.)

7. The Muster Gate near the northeastern corner where the guard likely gathered

8. The Sheep Gate on the northern wall where sacrificial animals passed through

9. The Fish Gate on the northern wall leading to the fish market stocked with catch from the Sea of Galilee

10. The Old Gate on the northwestern wall (literally "Gate of the Old Wall")

Jerusalem's Dung Gate today

11. The Gate of Ephraim on the northwestern wall leading northwest toward Ephraim or Samaria

12. The Corner Gate on the northwestern corner of the wall

Related passages: Nehemiah 3:13–32; 12:31–39

3:9, 12–18 Distinct Districts

Nehemiah made an unusual comment in Nehemiah 3:9 — he referenced Rephaiah as the "official of half the district of Jerusalem." Later, Nehemiah identified Shallum as the official of the other "half district of Jerusalem" (Nehemiah 3:12). Jerusalem wasn't a large city at that time, so what were these districts, and what function did these officials serve?

The word *district* has four distinct functions in the Bible. It can refer to:

1. A section of land with distinct boundaries distinguished by tribal customs, a province within a country, or part of a province

2. A region around a city or a territory under the influence of that city

3. A tract of land holy to the Lord

4. An administrative or governmental district

Nehemiah 3 employs the fourth meaning. Following the custom of the Persian government, Nehemiah had divided the province of Judah into administrative districts, each with an established leader. Rephaniah and Shallum administered the primary district, Jerusalem. The other districts included these cities:

- Beth-haccerem — a village situated between Jerusalem and Bethlehem, administered by Malchijah. Jeremiah identified Beth-haccerem as a strategic point to spot signal fires (Jeremiah 6:1).

- Mizpah — a city on the border between the old kingdoms of Judah and Israel, administered by another Shallum. *Mizpah* means "lookout."

- Beth-zur — a city southwest of Jerusalem near Hebron, administered in part by another person named Nehemiah. Beth-zur was an important fortress along the Hebron-Jerusalem road.

- Keilah—an elevated city (1,500 feet above sea level) just northwest of Beth-zur, administered by Rehum and Bavvai. During the
time of Saul and David, Keilah boasted protective gates and bars
(1 Samuel 23:7).

Related passages: Ezekiel 4:1–8; Matthew 4:13; 19:1; Mark 8:10; Acts 16:12

5:1–11   Ancient Loan Sharks

Economic depression can threaten a nation at any time. In post-exile
Jerusalem, the people rebuilding the city suffered a great depression. The
landless suffered food shortages (Nehemiah 5:2). Landlords mortgaged
their land because of famine (5:3). And just about everyone borrowed
money to pay Persian taxes (5:4).

Some of the escaped captives even sold their children into slavery
to settle debts (5:5). The Law would have accounted for these children
under its prescription that Israelites who sold themselves into slavery
to their countrymen were to be treated as hired hands and never resold
to foreigners. After six years of service, such slaves were to be freed
(Exodus 21:1–6). But this was not upheld in Judah immediately after
the return from Babylonian captivity. Nehemiah himself had bought back
Jews from foreign masters (Nehemiah 5:8). No wonder he was angry
(5:6).

Nehemiah was also angry because Israelites with means had loaned
money to their fellow citizens with interest (5:7). The Law, however,
stipulated that money should be lent to the poor—and to all fellow
Israelites—without interest (Exodus 22:25–27). So, Nehemiah commanded that all lands held in pledge of debts be returned and interest
charges forgiven, freeing up the people to pay off the principle of their
debts (Nehemiah 5:10–11).

*Related passages: Leviticus 25:35–46; Deuteronomy 24:10–13; 2 Kings 4:1;
Isaiah 50:1*

5:13   Rejected with a Dramatic Gesture

Every culture develops peculiar customs to express displeasure or rejection. In the modern-day West, people spit or curse, while in ancient Rome, they might have washed their hands, as Pontius Pilate did when the crowds demanded Jesus's death. Jews had at least two gestures to express their displeasure: shaking the dust off their feet and shaking out their robes.

Nehemiah "shook out the front of [his] garment" as a sign of displeasure and rejection of those who refused to follow his command to restore persons, lands, and houses to those who had sold them to pay off debts (Nehemiah 5:7–11). Nehemiah followed this dramatic gesture with a curse: "May God shake out every man from his house and from his possessions who does not fulfill this promise; even thus may he be shaken out and emptied" (5:13).

Related passages: Matthew 27:24; Luke 9:5; Acts 18:6

ESTHER

1:1 Ahasuerus=Xerxes?

The book of Esther begins in the throne room of a Persian king called
Ahasuerus, a name that comes into English from the Old Persian by
way of Babylonian and Hebrew. Most of the rest of history identifies the
Persian king at the center of Esther as Xerxes, which also comes from the
Old Persian but by way of Greek.

By combining the Bible's record of Ahasuerus with history's rendering
of Xerxes, a most distinctive personality arises. Lacking both the political
and military talents of his predecessors Cyrus II and Darius I, Ahasuerus
led his military deep into Greece. To get from Asia into Greece, Xerxes
ordered his engineers to build a bridge across the Hellespont. When
storms destroyed the bridge while it was still under construction, the
short-tempered Xerxes ordered his engineers beheaded. Once in Greece,
Xerxes' army and navy suffered tragic defeats on land (Plataea) and on
water (Mycale). Even worse, both defeats were on the same day. After
these defeats, Xerxes abandoned his army in Greece, leaving it to one of
his generals, and returned to his capital cities, Susa and Persepolis, where
he worked on construction projects.

Related passages: Ezra 4:6; Daniel 9:1

1:3 The Land of Persia

The area and people of ancient Persia identify most closely in today's
world with the modern-day nation of Iran. Located at the far eastern
edge of a populated and cultivated area called the Fertile Crescent, Persia

rose to international prominence only after 1000 BC. The Persians first show up in the historical records of Assyrians in the ninth century BC, when King Shalmaneser deported them and their neighbors, the Medes. Good relations existed between the Medes and the Persians until 549 BC when Cyrus II, the king of Persia, began to expand his territory near the Persian Gulf to the north and west, gaining control of Median lands. Within ten years, Cyrus II had created the largest empire yet in that part of the world. Two generations later, under Darius, the Persian Empire reached its height as Darius established a complex network of roads, placed faithful government officials throughout the empire, and refitted or built two new capitals: Susa and Persepolis. One final Persian leader of note, Xerxes, attempted to deal with problems on the Persia-Greece border only to experience a series of disastrous defeats. From then on, the Persian Empire declined until taken over by the Greeks under Alexander the Great in 331 BC.

Related passages: Ezra 1:1; Daniel 5:28

1:6   Royal Furniture

King Ahasuerus outfitted his palace at Susa with all manner of luxuries—among them couches of gold and silver. The terms *couch* and *bed* refer to similar objects in the biblical record, which often offers little to describe the specific differences between the two. Beds in the biblical era were sometimes short (Isaiah 28:20) and sometimes raised (2 Kings 1:4). Couches such as those in the palace of Ahasuerus were outfitted with precious materials, including gold and silver (Esther 1:6) as well as ivory (Amos 6:4). Such rich furnishings would not have been common among the people. Commoners who had access to similar types of furniture would have had plain, wood-framed versions. Couches could be used for beautifying oneself (Ezekiel 23:41); for taking meals, as the people at Ahasuerus's palace did; and for more personal encounters between husband and wife (Song of Solomon 1:16).

Related passages: Esther 7:8; Job 7:13

1:6   Building a Mosaic

Mosaics stand as one of the chief art forms to come out of the ancient world. The oldest mosaics date from before 3000 BC in Mesopotamia. Constructed from small pieces of colored stone, glass, jewels, or shells, mosaics served as walls or floors in ancient palaces and other buildings. To create a mosaic, craftsmen placed a variety of colored materials in certain patterns or designs. The art form continued into the Roman period, where it reached its height

Mosaic at Tabgha, Israel, in the Church of the Multiplication of the Loaves and Fishes

when craftsmen incorporated fine glass and gold into their designs. One especially significant ancient mosaic has been preserved at Tabgha in an ancient church where Byzantine Christians commemorated Jesus's feeding of the 5,000.

2:3   Ancient Fashion

Although cosmetics appear only rarely in Scripture, they were widely available in the ancient world. Eye paints, powders, and rouges were developed from minerals and ochers in a variety of colors, especially green, black, and red. Ointments and perfumes were developed from oils and animal fats and were used not just for adornment but also to change the color of the skin, nails, and hair. The ancients also used ointments and perfumes for burials.

Archaeologists have discovered a number of implements that the ancients used to hold and apply cosmetics—limestone bowls for paints, small burned-black jugs for perfumes, and ivory or alabaster jars for ointments (Luke 7:37). Those applying cosmetics would have used mirrors, common items in the biblical era.

The Bible mentions cosmetics in a neutral way regarding Esther's preparations to meet King Ahasuerus (Esther 2:3). At other times, the Bible offers a negative perspective—such as in cosmetics' connection with Judah's idolatry and faithlessness (Jeremiah 4:30)—or a positive perspective—as in the context of Solomon's marriage (Song of Solomon 3:6).

Related passages: Song of Solomon 1:13; Ezekiel 23:40

2:3   The Varied Fates of Eunuchs

Eunuchs show up early in biblical and historical records. The origin of the practice—male castration—while certainly not Jewish, remains unknown. However, Moses acknowledged the presence of eunuchs in Deuteronomy 23:1, excluding them from the worship of the Israelites. This exclusion suggests castration originated in pagan communities, and certainly, castration stripped a man of his ability to fulfill God's first command to humanity: "Be fruitful and multiply" (Genesis 1:28). Though the Law kept eunuchs from worshiping with God's people, the role of eunuchs in pagan society expanded as the centuries passed. Kings often placed eunuchs in key positions of power or influence, for people in general believed that eunuchs were more singly focused on their work. This led to eunuchs being appointed as military leaders, government officials, and seen most often in Scripture, as overseers of the king's harem (Esther 2:3). Early Christians were divided over the question of eunuchs, due to differing interpretations of Matthew 19:12, but by the fourth century AD, the practice was strongly discouraged.

Related passages: Esther 1:10; 6:2

4:11 The Royal Scepter

A king's scepter symbolized the power and authority that came with his position. The ancients constructed these rods or staffs out of fine metals such as gold. Ancient depictions of royal or deistic figures often portray individual rulers with scepters, some as long as approximately four feet, others as short as one or two feet. The shorter scepters have their roots in ancient weaponry, particularly the mace. Such scepters symbolized not just power but also judgment or oppression.

The Bible draws upon a royal tradition of extending the scepter, particularly in the book of Esther, which records the way Xerxes used his scepter to deal with his subjects (Esther 4:11; 5:2; 8:4). This tradition of extending the scepter indicated the king's power to grant all manner of privilege — from a simple hearing with him to the power to rule a kingdom. The prophetic books use the image of a broken scepter to illustrate

God's breaking the power of disobedient kings (Jeremiah 48:17). The psalms also pick up the scepter imagery, calling Judah — God's people ruling on His behalf — His scepter (Psalm 60:7). Also in the psalms, we see God pictured as a king extending His scepter as He grants the Messiah the authority to rule (110:2).

Egyptian corner relief fragment with an image of the deities Mehyet and Onuris-Shu, both of whom hold scepters

Related passages: Psalm 45:6; Zechariah 10:11

6:1 Reading in the Ancient World

Though literacy was spotty in the ancient world, as a religion of the Book, Judaism placed a great emphasis on reading. As far back as the post-exilic sixth century BC, families in general sustained this emphasis by teaching their boys to read Hebrew so they would have the ability

Torah (scroll)

to study the Torah. The Jewish tradition of public reading extends back even further to Moses's reading the covenant aloud to the people at Sinai (Exodus 24:7). This reading of the Law set a pattern for Jewish and Christian practice in the following centuries, as reading aloud from Scripture became standard in public religious gatherings (Jeremiah 36:6). In synagogues, the practice evolved, allowing any man present—not only leaders—to read Scripture aloud, as Jesus did on occasion (Luke 4:16). Further, after synagogue readings, those present were called upon to comment, an opportunity Paul used to preach the gospel to those gathered (Acts 13:15–42).

The emphasis on private reading and study was also strong throughout Jewish and Christian tradition, at least among the religious leadership (2 Timothy 4:13). Interestingly, in the ancient world, even private reading occurred audibly. When people read to themselves, they often read aloud, explaining why Philip could overhear the Ethiopian eunuch reading to himself (Acts 8:30). Kings, with the abundant resources at their disposal, could afford personal readers (Esther 6:1).

Related passages: Nehemiah 8:3; 1 Timothy 4:13

9:3   Government in the Persian Empire

Persian ruler Darius I created the governmental position of satrap so
he might have someone to assist him in administering his empire.
Daniel 6:1 mentions 120 satraps in the empire, though that number
could have included a variety of government officials. Satraps, appointed
by the king, ruled over smaller, more manageable segments of the empire
called satrapies. Satraps reported directly to the king and had their own
courts and officials. However, while satraps held ultimate power in their
regions, they worked with other officials also appointed by and reporting
to the king. This strategy set in place by the Persian kings prevented any
one satrap from attempting a rebellion in his satrapy and contributed to
the stability of the empire.

Related passages: Ezra 8:36; Daniel 3:2

9:17   A Celebration of Deliverance

The festival of Purim finds its roots in Esther's redemptive story. When
Haman planned to annihilate the Jews, he cast lots to find the ideal
day. A game of chance believed to discern the will of the gods, casting
lots resembled rolling dice (Jonah 1:7). When Haman cast his lots, also
called *pur*, they fell on the thirteenth day of Adar (February–March, see
Esther 9:1). But on that day, God delivered the Jews from annihilation
and the *pur* became a symbol of divine protection. On the day after the
Jews' deliverance from the Persian holocaust, Mordecai established an
annual celebration. This memorial occurs every year during a two-day
festival called Purim, derived from the Hebrew word *pur* (Esther 9:18).
On the thirteenth of Adar, the Jewish community observes a solemn fast
and reads the book of Esther out loud, blotting out Haman's name. On
the fourteenth, a celebration begins by breaking the fast with a feast. The
people spend the rest of the fourteenth and all of the fifteenth feasting,
celebrating, and giving gifts.

Related Passages: Esther 3:7; 9:19–22

APPENDIX

HOW TO BEGIN A RELATIONSHIP WITH GOD

The Bible retains its relevance in all cultures and communities. The message of Scripture speaks to all people because all people have been created by God in His image, all people have fallen from the original state of glory, and all people are in need of God's salvation through Jesus. The Bible marks the path to Him with four essential truths. Let's look at each marker in detail.

Our Spiritual Condition: Totally Depraved

The first truth is rather personal. One look in the mirror of Scripture, and our human condition becomes painfully clear:

> "There is none righteous, not even one;
> There is none who understands,
> There is none who seeks for God;
> All have turned aside, together they have become useless;
> There is none who does good,
> There is not even one." (Romans 3:10–12)

We are all sinners through and through—totally depraved. Now, that doesn't mean we've committed every atrocity known to humankind. We're not as *bad* as we can be, just as *bad off* as we can be. Sin colors all our thoughts, motives, words, and actions.

If you've been around a while, you likely already believe it. Look around. Everything around us bears the smudge marks of our sinful nature. Despite our best efforts to create a perfect world, crime statistics continue to soar, divorce rates keep climbing, and families keep crumbling.

Something has gone terribly wrong in our society and in ourselves—something deadly. Contrary to how the world would repackage it, "me-first" living doesn't equal rugged individuality and freedom; it equals death. As Paul said in his letter to the Romans, "The wages of sin is death" (Romans 6:23)—our spiritual and physical death that comes from God's righteous judgment of our sin, along with all of the emotional and practical effects of this separation that we experience on a daily basis. This brings us to the second marker: God's character.

God's Character: Infinitely Holy

How can God judge us for a sinful state we were born into? Our total depravity is only half the answer. The other half is God's infinite holiness.

The fact that we know things are not as they should be points us to a standard of goodness beyond ourselves. Our sense of injustice in life on this side of eternity implies a perfect standard of justice beyond our reality. That standard and source is God Himself. And God's standard of holiness contrasts starkly with our sinful condition.

Scripture says that "God is Light, and in Him there is no darkness at all" (1 John 1:5). God is absolutely holy—which creates a problem for us. If He is so pure, how can we who are so impure relate to Him?

Perhaps we could try being better people, try to tilt the balance in favor of our good deeds, or seek out methods for self-improvement. Throughout history, people have attempted to live up to God's standard by keeping the Ten Commandments or living by their own code of ethics. Unfortunately, no one can come close to satisfying the demands of God's law. Romans 3:20 says, "By the works of the Law no flesh will be justified in His sight; for through the Law comes the knowledge of sin."

Our Need: A Substitute

So here we are, sinners by nature and sinners by choice, trying to pull ourselves up by our own bootstraps to attain a relationship with our holy Creator. But every time we try, we fall flat on our faces. We can't live a good enough life to make up for our sin, because God's standard isn't "good enough"—it's *perfection*. And we can't make amends for the offense our sin has created without dying for it.

Who can get us out of this mess?

If someone could live perfectly, honoring God's law, and would bear sin's death penalty for us—in our place—then we would be saved from our predicament. But is there such a person? Thankfully, yes!

Meet your substitute—*Jesus Christ*. He is the One who took death's place for you!

> [God] made [Jesus Christ] who knew no sin to be sin on our behalf, so that we might become the righteousness of God in Him. (2 Corinthians 5:21)

God's Provision: A Savior

God rescued us by sending His Son, Jesus, to die on the cross for our sins (1 John 4:9–10). Jesus was fully human and fully divine (John 1:1, 18), a truth that ensures His understanding of our weaknesses, His power to forgive, and His ability to bridge the gap between God and us (Romans 5:6–11). In short, we are "justified as a gift by His grace through the redemption which is in Christ Jesus" (Romans 3:24). Two words in this verse bear further explanation: *justified* and *redemption*.

Justification is God's act of mercy, in which He declares righteous the believing sinners while we are still in our sinning state. Justification doesn't mean that God *makes* us righteous, so that we never sin again, rather that He *declares* us righteous—much like a judge pardons a guilty criminal. Because Jesus took our sin upon Himself and suffered our judgment on the cross, God forgives our debt and proclaims us PARDONED.

Redemption is Christ's act of paying the complete price to release us from sin's bondage. God sent His Son to bear His wrath for all of our sins—past, present, and future (Romans 3:24–26; 2 Corinthians 5:21). In humble obedience, Christ willingly endured the shame of the cross for our sake (Mark 10:45; Romans 5:6–8; Philippians 2:8). Christ's death satisfied God's righteous demands. He no longer holds our sins against us, because His own Son paid the penalty for them. We are freed from the slave market of sin, never to be enslaved again!

Placing Your Faith in Christ

These four truths describe how God has provided a way to Himself through Jesus Christ. Because the price has been paid in full by God, we must respond to His free gift of eternal life in total faith and confidence in Him to save us. We must step forward into the relationship with God that He has prepared for us—not by doing good works or by being a good person, but by coming to Him just as we are and accepting His justification and redemption by faith.

> For by grace you have been saved through faith; and that not of yourselves, it is the gift of God; not as a result of works, so that no one may boast. (Ephesians 2:8–9)

We accept God's gift of salvation simply by placing our faith in Christ alone for the forgiveness of our sins. Would you like to enter a relationship with your Creator by trusting in Christ as your Savior? If so, here's a simple prayer you can use to express your faith:

> *Dear God,*
>
> *I know that my sin has put a barrier between You and me. Thank You for sending Your Son, Jesus, to die in my place. I trust in Jesus alone to forgive my sins, and I accept His gift of eternal life. I ask Jesus to be my personal Savior and the Lord of my life. Thank You. In Jesus's name, amen.*

If you've prayed this prayer or one like it and you wish to find out more about knowing God and His plan for you in the Bible, contact us at Insight for Living Ministries. Our contact information is on the following pages.

WE ARE HERE FOR YOU

If you desire to find out more about knowing God and His plan for you in the Bible, contact us. Insight for Living Ministries provides staff pastors who are available for free written correspondence or phone consultation. These seminary-trained and seasoned counselors have years of experience and are well-qualified guides for your spiritual journey.

Please feel welcome to contact your regional office by using the information below:

United States
Insight for Living
Biblical Counseling Department
Post Office Box 269000
Plano, Texas 75026-9000
USA
972-473-5097, Monday through Friday,
8:00 a.m. – 5:00 p.m. central time
www.insight.org/contactapastor

Canada
Insight for Living Canada
Biblical Counseling Department
PO Box 8 Stn A
Abbotsford BC V2T 6Z4
CANADA
1-800-663-7639
info@insightforliving.ca

Australia, New Zealand, and South Pacific
Insight for Living Australia
Pastoral Care
Post Office Box 443
Boronia, VIC 3155
AUSTRALIA
1300 467 444

United Kingdom and Europe
Insight for Living United Kingdom
Pastoral Care
PO Box 553
Dorking
RH4 9EU
UNITED KINGDOM
0800 787 9364
+44 (0)1306 640156
pastoralcare@insightforliving.org.uk

ENDNOTES

Deuteronomy

1. Earl S. Kalland, "Deuteronomy," in *The Expositor's Bible Commentary*, vol. 3, *Deuteronomy, Joshua, Judges, Ruth, 1 & 2 Samuel*, gen. ed. Frank E. Gaebelein (Grand Rapids: Zondervan, 1992), 66.

2. Steven Barabas, "Door," in *The Zondervan Pictorial Encyclopedia of the Bible*, vol. 2, *D–G*, gen. ed. Merrill C. Tenney (Grand Rapids: Zondervan, 1976), 155.

3. Kalland, "Deuteronomy," in *The Expositor's Bible Commentary*, vol. 3, 91.

4. J. C. DeYoung, "Gerizim," in *The Zondervan Pictorial Encyclopedia of the Bible*, vol. 2, *D–G*, 701–703.

5. Kalland, "Deuteronomy," in *The Expositor's Bible Commentary*, vol. 3, 100–101.

6. K. A. Kitchen, "Canaan, Canaanites," in *New Bible Dictionary*, 2nd ed., ed. J. D. Douglas and others (Wheaton, Ill.: Tyndale House, 1987), 166.

7. Kalland, "Deuteronomy," in *The Expositor's Bible Commentary*, vol. 3, 135, 136.

8. Jack S. Deere, "Deuteronomy," in *The Bible Knowledge Commentary, Old Testament*, ed. John F. Walvoord and Roy B. Zuck (Wheaton, Ill.: Victor Books, 1986), 299.

9. G. S. Cansdale, "Cattle," in *The Zondervan Pictorial Encyclopedia of the Bible*, vol. 1, *A–C*, 765–66.

10. Guy B. Funderburk, "Threshing," in *The Zondervan Pictorial Encyclopedia of the Bible*, vol. 5, *Q–Z*, 738–39.

11. H. L. Ellison, "Witness," in *New Bible Dictionary*, 2nd ed., 1258.

12. F. C. Fensham, "Covenant, Alliance," in *New Bible Dictionary*, 2nd ed., 240–42.

Joshua

1. Joel F. Drinkard, Jr., "Cities," in *Harper's Bible Dictionary*, gen. ed. Paul J. Achtemeier (San Francisco: Harper & Row, 1985), 172.

2. D. G. Burke, "Home," in *The International Standard Bible Encyclopedia*, vol. 2, *E–J*, ed. Geoffrey W. Bromiley and others (Grand Rapids: Eerdmans, 1987), 747–48.

3. A. C. Dickie and J. B. Payne, "House," in *The International Standard Bible Encyclopedia*, vol. 2, *E–J*, 771–72.

4. Perdue, Leo G., *Wisdom Literature: A Theological History* (Louisville: Westminster John Knox, 2007), 100–101, accessed on Google Books http://books.google.com/books?id=AN9lxYT0ZGUC&pg=PA100&lpg=PA100&dq=role+of+pagan+priests+in+ancient+near+east+warfare&source=bl&ots=Gm4mAew8GB&sig=4z6kBMVpah7BufNKpLcMMxAGTkE&hl=en&sa=X&ei=ZpeT6blOujA2gW678mzDw&ved=0CB4Q6AEwAA#v=onepage&q=role%20of%20pagan%20priests%20in%20ancient%20near%20east%20warfare&f=false (accessed Feb. 13, 2013).

5. R. P. Gordon, "War," in *New Bible Dictionary*, 2nd ed., ed. J. D. Douglas and others (Wheaton, Ill.: Tyndale House, 1987), 1241.

6. Donald H. Madvig, "Joshua," in *The Expositor's Bible Commentary*, vol. 3, *Deuteronomy, Joshua, Judges, Ruth, 1 & 2 Samuel*, gen. ed. Frank E. Gaebelein (Grand Rapids: Zondervan, 1992), 266.

7. Merrill F. Unger, "Canaan, Canaanites," in *The New Unger's Bible Dictionary*, ed. R. K. Harrison (Chicago: Moody Press, 1988), 202.

8. Unger, "Canaan, Canaanites," in *The New Unger's Bible Dictionary*, 202–203.

9. Merrill F. Unger and Howard F. Vos, "Hittites," in *The New Unger's Bible Dictionary*, 576, 579.

10. "Hivites," in *The New Unger's Bible Dictionary*, 580.

11. W. Haskell and Merrill F. Unger, "Perizzites," in *The New Unger's Bible Dictionary*, 986.

12. "Girgashites," in *The New Unger's Bible Dictionary*, 477.

13. Herbert B. Huffmon, "Amorites," in *Harper's Bible Dictionary*, 27.

14. "Jebusite, Jebusites," in *The New Unger's Bible Dictionary*, 655.

15. D. R. Bowes, "Flint," in *The Zondervan Pictorial Encyclopedia of the Bible*, vol. 2, *D–G*, gen. ed. Merrill C. Tenney (Grand Rapids: Zondervan, 1976), 549–50.

16. All info in this section is based on K. N. Schoville, "War," in *The International Standard Bible Encyclopedia*, vol. 4, *Q–Z*, ed. Geoffrey W. Bromiley and others (Grand Rapids: Eerdmans, 1988), 1016–17.

17. K. N. Schoville, "Seige," in *The International Standard Bible Encyclopedia*, vol. 4, *Q–Z*, 503.

18. J. K. Hoffmeier, "Weapons of War," in *The International Standard Bible Encyclopedia*, vol. 4, *Q–Z*, 1036.

19. "Armor, Arms," in *The New Unger's Bible Dictionary*, 104–105; [J. K. Hoffmeier, "Weapons of War," in *The International Standard Bible Encyclopedia*, vol. 4, *Q–Z*, 1038.]

20. "Armor, Arms," in *The New Unger's Bible Dictionary*, 105.

21. E. M. Blaiklock, "Altar," in *The Zondervan Pictorial Encyclopedia of the Bible*, vol. 1, *A–C*, 119.

22. "Altar," in *The New Unger's Bible Dictionary*, 49.

23. *The Book of Jasher*, 88:63–65, reprint of photo lithographic, reprint of exact ed. (Salt Lake City: J. H. Parry, 1887), http://www.ccel.org/a/anonymous/jasher/88.htm (accessed Feb. 13, 2013).

24. A. C. Schultz, "Jarimoth/Jashobeam," in *The Zondervan Pictorial Encyclopedia of the Bible*, vol. 3, *H–L*, 407.

25. A. van Selms, "Book of Jashar," in *The New Bible Dictionary*, 2nd ed., 552.

26. James Orr and R. K. Harrison, "Book of Jashar," in *The International Standard Bible Encyclopedia*, vol. 2, *E–J*, 969.

First Samuel

1. Flavius Josephus, "The Wars of the Jews," IV.vii.2, *The Works of Flavius Josephus*, trans. William Whiston (Auburn and Buffalo: John E. Beardsley, 1895), http://www.perseus.tufts.edu/hopper/text?doc=Perseus:text:1999.01.0148 (accessed May 18, 2012).

Second Samuel

1.   Ronald F. Youngblood, "1, 2 Samuel," in *The Expositor's Bible Commentary*, vol. 3, *Deuteronomy, Joshua, Judges, Ruth, 1 & 2 Samuel*, gen. ed. Frank E. Gaebelein (Grand Rapids: Zondervan, 1992), 811.

2.   Youngblood, "1, 2 Samuel," in *The Expositor's Bible Commentary*, vol. 3, 874.

3.   E. B. Johnston, "Dance," in *The International Standard Bible Encyclopedia*, vol. 1, *A–D*, ed. Geoffrey W. Bromiley and others (Grand Rapids: Eerdmans, 1988), 856–57.

4.   W. J. Cameron, "Shaving," in *The Zondervan Pictorial Encyclopedia of the Bible*, vol. 5, *Q–Z*, gen. ed. Merrill C. Tenney (Grand Rapids: Zondervan, 1976), 378.

5.   R. K. Harrison, "Beard," in *The International Standard Bible Encyclopedia*, vol. 1, *A–D*, 442.

6.   W. White, Jr., "Bath, Bathe, Bathing," in *The Zondervan Pictorial Encyclopedia of the Bible*, vol. 1, *A–C*, 490.

7.   Merrill F. Unger, "Bathe, Bathing," in *The New Unger's Bible Dictionary*, ed. R. K. Harrison (Chicago: Moody Press, 1988), 149.

8.   Youngblood, "1, 2 Samuel," in *The Expositor's Bible Commentary*, vol. 3, 929.

9.   K. N. Schoville, "War," in *The International Standard Bible Encyclopedia*, vol. 4, *Q–Z*, ed. Geoffrey W. Bromiley and others (Grand Rapids: Eerdmans, 1988), 1016.

Second Kings

1.   E. E. Carpenter, "Sacrifice, Human," in *The International Standard Bible Encyclopedia*, vol. 4, *Q–Z*, ed. Geoffrey W. Bromiley and others (Grand Rapids: Eerdmans, 1988), 259.

2.   P. E. Adolph, "Healing, Health," in *The Zondervan Pictorial Encyclopedia of the Bible*, vol. 3, *H–L*, gen. ed. Merrill C. Tenney (Grand Rapids: Zondervan, 1976), 55.

3.   C. G. Rasmussen, "Naaman," in *The International Standard Bible Encyclopedia*, vol. 3, *K–P*, ed. Geoffrey W. Bromiley and others (Grand Rapids: Eerdmans, 1987), 465.

4.   John H. Walton, Victor Harold Matthews, Mark W. Chavalas, *The IVP Bible Background Commentary: Old Testament* (Downers Grove, Ill.: InterVarsity, 2000), 548.

5.   "Carites," in *The International Standard Bible Encyclopedia*, vol. 1, *A–D*, ed. Geoffrey W. Bromiley and others (Grand Rapids: Eerdmans, 1988), 618.

6.   J. L. Kelso, "Samaritans," in *The Zondervan Pictorial Encyclopedia of the Bible*, vol. 5, *Q–Z*, 244–45.

7.   Thomas L. Constable, "2 Kings," in *The Bible Knowledge Commentary: Old Testament*, ed. John F. Walvoord and Roy B. Zuck (Wheaton, Ill.: Victor Books, 1986), 573.

8.   Merrill F. Unger, "Amulet," in *The New Unger's Bible Dictionary*, ed. R. K. Harrison (Chicago: Moody Press, 1988), 56.

9.   Merrill F. Unger, "Shallum," in *The New Unger's Bible Dictionary*, 1166.

10. G. V. Smith, "Prophet," in *The International Standard Bible Encyclopedia*, vol. 3, *K–P*, 991–92.

11. D. G. Schley, "Sun," and M. Liverani, trans. W. S. LaSor, "Ugarit," in *The International Standard Bible Encyclopedia*, vol. 4, *Q–Z*, 663, 937.

12. S. Barabas, "Vassal," in *The Zondervan Pictorial Encyclopedia of the Bible*, vol. 5, *Q–Z*, gen. ed. Merrill C. Tenney (Grand Rapids: Zondervan, 1976), 862.

Second Chronicles

1.   Nola J. Opperwall-Galluch, "Shemaiah," in *The International Standard Bible Encyclopedia*, vol. 4, *Q–Z*, ed. Geoffrey W. Bromiley and others (Grand Rapids: Eerdmans, 1988), 470.

2.   Philip Wendell Crannell, "Iddo," in *The International Standard Bible Encyclopedia*, vol. 2, *E–J*, ed. Geoffrey W. Bromiley and others (Grand Rapids: Eerdmans, 1987), 793.

3.   Gary V. Smith, "Prophet," in *The International Standard Bible Encyclopedia*, vol. 3, *K–P*, ed. Geoffrey Bromiley and others (Grand Rapids: Eerdmans, 1987), 986–89.

4.   Eugene H. Merrill, "2 Chronicles," in *The Bible Knowledge Commentary: Old Testament*, ed. John F. Walvoord and Roy B. Zuck (Wheaton, Ill.: Victor, 1986), 631.

5.   Opperwall-Galluch, "Zerah," in *The International Standard Bible Encyclopedia*, vol. 4, *Q–Z*, 1192.

6.   Burton MacDonald, "Edom," in *The International Standard Bible Encyclopedia*, vol. 2, *E–J*, 20.

7.   Victor H. Matthews, "Waterworks," in *The International Standard Bible Encyclopedia*, vol. 4, *Q–Z*, 1029–30.

8.   Donn F. Morgan, "Captivity," in *The International Standard Bible Encyclopedia*, vol. 1, *A–D*, ed. Geoffrey W. Bromiley and others (Grand Rapids: Eerdmans, 1988), 613.

RESOURCES FOR PROBING FURTHER

The Old Testament is filled with details of long-ago life that sound foreign to our modern-day ears. Thankfully, numerous resources give twenty-first-century readers the insight we need to understand the details of the ancient Book. Here, we have listed several such resources for you. Keep in mind that we cannot always endorse everything a writer or ministry says, so we encourage you to approach these and all other non-biblical resources with wisdom and discernment.

Arnold, Clinton E., and others, eds. *Zondervan Illustrated Bible Backgrounds Commentary*, 4 vols. Grand Rapids: Zondervan, 2002.

Bromiley, Geoffrey W., ed. *The International Standard Bible Encyclopedia*, 4 vols. Grand Rapids: Eerdmans, 1995.

Insight for Living. *Insight's Old Testament Handbook: A Practical Look at Each Book*. Plano, Tex.: IFL Publishing House, 2010.

Marshall, I. Howard, and others, eds. *New Bible Dictionary*, 3d ed. Downers Grove, Ill.: InterVarsity, 1996.

Packer, J. I., and M. C. Tenney, eds. *Illustrated Manners and Customs of the Bible*. Nashville: Thomas Nelson, 1980.

Walvoord, John F., and Roy B. Zuck, eds. *The Bible Knowledge Commentary: An Exposition of the Scriptures by Dallas Seminary Faculty, Old Testament Edition*. Wheaton, Ill.: Victor Books, 1986.

ORDERING INFORMATION

If you would like to order additional copies of *Insight's Handbook of Old Testament Backgrounds: Key Customs from Each Book, Genesis – Esther* or other Insight for Living Ministries' resources, please contact the office that serves you.

United States

Insight for Living
Post Office Box 269000
Plano, Texas 75026-9000
USA
1-800-772-8888
Monday through Friday,
7:00 a.m. – 7:00 p.m. central time
www.insight.org
www.insightworld.org

Canada

Insight for Living Canada
PO Box 8 Stn A
Abbotsford BC V2T 6Z4
CANADA
1-800-663-7639
www.insightforliving.ca

Australia, New Zealand, and South Pacific

Insight for Living Australia
Post Office Box 443
Boronia, VIC 3155
AUSTRALIA
1300 467 444
www.insight.asn.au

United Kingdom and Europe

Insight for Living United Kingdom
PO Box 553
Dorking
RH4 9EU
UNITED KINGDOM
0800 787 9364
www.insightforliving.org.uk

Other International Locations

International constituents may contact the U.S. office through our
Web site (www.insightworld.org), mail queries, or by calling
+1-972-473-5136.

SCRIPTURE INDEX

Exodus

Leviticus

Numbers

Deuteronomy

Ruth

1 Samuel

2 Samuel

1 Kings

2 Kings

1 Chronicles

2 Chronicles

Ezra

Nehemiah

Esther

Jeremiah

Ezekiel

Daniel

NEW TESTAMENT

SUBJECT INDEX